Never Wanted;
Always *Needed*

Allowing Life's Hardships and Heartaches
to Bring You to Your Purpose

Sarah Lee

WESTBOW
P R E S S®
A DIVISION OF THOMAS NELSON
& ZONDERVAN

WestBow Press books may be ordered through booksellers or by contacting:

WestBow Press
A Division of Thomas Nelson & Zondervan
1663 Liberty Drive
Bloomington, IN 47403
www.westbowpress.com
1 (866) 928-1240

ISBN: 978-1-9736-8316-2 (sc)
ISBN: 978-1-9736-8318-6 (hc)
ISBN: 978-1-9736-8317-9 (e)

Library of Congress Control Number: 2020900327

Print information available on the last page.

WestBow Press rev. date: 01/16/2020

To the woman whose life is
not anywhere she envisioned it to be.
Let us hold hands as we embrace the
unimaginable and navigate through
the hardships of life that knock us down.
Let us discover our purpose.

Contents

Preface

Five years ago, as I dropped my kids off at school and drove the fifteen minutes to work, I cried. This became a daily occurrence. I was so unhappy in life. This fifteen-minute drive became a very special time with God where I continually cried out asking Him to change things. I pleaded with God to use me to impact the lives of others so that they may see His light amidst whatever it might be. I pleaded with Him to help me find happiness somewhere in my life. How was I to continue like this for the rest of my life? As I came to the bridge that I cross daily, *write a book* came to mind. "Umm, no!" was my immediate answer. I cannot even speak words well, much less write them. Over the next few years, people would stop me or send me messages encouraging me to write a book because of posts made on social media or a letter I had written to the church. My answer was still no. People would continue making statements about how good I am with my words. I would push the thoughts away. I had just recently found a love for reading but had no desire to tell my story. As I read others' stories and learned from their wisdom, those stories helped me during the hardest years of my life. As writing kept being placed on my heart, I decided to embrace it and just see where it would lead me. I have become completely vulnerable with my story. My prayer is that this book finds someone just where I have been and gives them courage and strength to continue going. I pray this book allows you to call "your" story yours and not be ashamed. I want to pray for you, my friend, and be somebody who can encourage you through the hard seasons of life. Find me on Instagram @the. sarah.lee, Facebook @the.sarah.lee.nwan, and the.sarah.lee.nwan@ gmail.com.

Introduction

D o you ever sit and wonder where your life has taken you? When the life you dreamed of and thought you would someday have is nothing but still a dream. Life is so far away from where or what you ever thought it would be.

Life has a way of taking us down roads that leave us in despair and wondering how in the world things can get better. Not knowing if you can make it through another day of heartbreak, nightmares, insecurities, self-destruction, crying, depression, addictions, and self-doubt.

Life has thrown curveballs that I never saw coming. I have made choices that deep down I knew the outcome but did not want to face the consequences. The unknown brings fear, as I want to know the end result to whatever it may be. Through all the heartbreak and the happiness that has occurred in my life, I choose to focus on the blessings even on the days when I don't feel blessed at all—when I feel like I've been cursed and I think I'm being punished for choices I have made in my past. I have finally come to the place in my life where I can say, "God's got this!"

It took a lot of heartbreak and being completely broken mentally, emotionally, and physically to get there, but without a doubt in my mind I know God's got this!

He has done things differently than the way I would have chosen. Seasons of life are nothing like I imagined they would be. I am learning to just surrender everything and let God take control. I may not understand it, and many times I do not like it, but He is working good through all of this for something or someone!

This has not been easy. The nights have been long. The walls have closed in. Miles have been walked. Tears have been cried. Sleep has been deprived.

You know the saying, "What doesn't kill you, makes you stronger." It is true. It is ultimately our own choosing whether we allow our past or even our present to kill us.

For some this may come easy, but for so many of us it is not. It has taken lots of soul searching, lots of heartache, and many tears. I was once a planner and what many would call OCD. I thrived on checklists and knowing what was expected, when it should be done, and how I was going to get there. As life continues to unfold, and especially through the last few years, I have discovered planning is overrated. At many times it leaves me with only disappointments and frustration.

I came to a point in my life where I found myself pondering on the question *What is my purpose here on this earth?*

My prayer and hope is that you, my friend, find encouragement and reassurance no matter where life has taken you. Find true love for yourself. Love the parts of you that you wish you could change—the parts that make you cringe. Embrace the choices of your life that leave you broken and ashamed. God is not done with you. The journey of life that you are on brings situations and emotions you never wanted, but it is the thing you need to lead you to your purpose in life.

Chapter 1

The Past

Exhaustion, anxiety, worry, anger, bitterness, loneliness, frustration, fear, nervousness, annoyed, overwhelmed, stuck, self-doubt, depression, addiction, despair. How many of these emotions do you struggle with? I have allowed these emotions to consume me throughout the years. I have allowed them to dictate the decisions I have made and to encompass my daily life.

It is so easy to fall into the brokenness that has impacted our lives. The brokenness that tells us we are not worthy of anything good in our lives. The brokenness fuels our doubt and insecurities and leaves us feeling hopeless. If you are feeling this way and are being suffocated by the weight of emotions from your past, know that you do not have to live like this.

We all have a past. I have failures, hurts, struggles, and hardships that make up my past. I allow my past to define who I am. I feel unworthy at times and feel as though I am failing at every task and obstacle thrown my way. I feel inadequate so many days. I am so afraid of making another mistake. I become paralyzed in my thoughts. I become stuck in the notion of being alone and feeling as though God is not even around.

I have allowed my past to keep me from living. Fear has a way of taking over and causing you to become stagnant. You do not want any more pain or sadness, so you choose to live isolated—isolated in your thoughts and decisions. You tell yourself you got yourself here, so you can get yourself out. This, my friend, is exactly where I found myself after years and years of trying to make life work out the way I had always imagined it would.

We must choose to embrace our past.

Maybe you have a past that is ugly. You have things that eat you alive and haunt you day in and day out. If people knew half the things you have done in your life, they would never look at you the same. People would leave you and go the other way, leaving you with a sense of loneliness and unworthiness.

Maybe people already know your past or even your present. They see and know who you truly are, and you are ashamed of the choices you have made in life. You are ashamed of what you have been dealt in life. Some of life's worst hardships do not fall on us because of choices we make. The hardship comes simply by living in a broken world—a broken world full of death, sickness, and even addiction that is out of our control. Those hardships that we are left to face and endure can lead us down a spiraling staircase. Hardships lead us to more hurt, rejection, betrayal, and sadness of our own choosing— especially when it becomes one thing after another. We play the blame game and become buried in self-pity.

I understand placing blame on others or on circumstances and feeling as though you have been dealt an unfair hand in life. I also can relate to feeling sorry for yourself and getting other people to feel sorry for you too, but what are we doing for others and ourselves when we place blame and wallow in our self-pity? Misery follows the one who seeks sympathy.

I do not want someone to have sympathy for me or feel sorry for me and the things I have gone through. If I am seeking sympathy from people, I will get a façade of responses that are not genuine. A person may show compassion but not be compassionate. I do not want them to feel pity for me. Kind words are uplifting, but being sympathetic is something we are "supposed to do." It does not take much work to be sympathetic. When someone does not understand or relate to your situation, it can become words just being said. When someone has no desire to try to understand or relate to your situation or feelings, it becomes just words as well. These words leave you feeling hopeless, unworthy, and all alone. Instead, I desire empathy. I want someone to truly desire to understand my world. I want someone to share the feelings I have encountered and with which I am dealing.

Being empathetic takes a lot more work. It requires effort. I strive to be empathetic with my students and the people that cross my path. I do not just want to say a simple phrase that everyone else says; I want them to see that I try to put myself in their shoes. I try to see where they are coming from and where their emotions are coming from. I take their feelings, their grief, their behavior into account. I must ask myself: *What would I feel if I ever had to endure such a thing? If I ever had to fight the battle? If I ever had to face the demon that has taken hold of their hearts, minds, and thoughts?*

It is easier for some to be more empathetic than sympathetic. They have seen and endured enough in life, so they can relate to someone's story and past. It may not be the same scenario they experienced, but they can relate. It is easier to be empathetic when someone is crying and his or her heart is broken. It is harder to be empathetic when anger, bitterness, and a bad attitude encompass the brokenhearted. Yet we all, at some point in our lives, have dealt with the same emotions. Maybe not the same circumstances, but we needed people to be empathetic for our emotions during our "fire," when life for us felt out of control and hopeless.

I compare my past to another's past thinking that my struggle or my heartbreak does not compare to the hurt and pain he or she has endured. I feel as though I have no reason to complain about my life. I have guilt that I have been given blessings they've never received. No matter how I want to categorize my past—good or bad, better or worse, pretty or ugly—I have to remember when I am in the midst of my own pain, abandonment, rejection, heartbreak, or struggle that it is just as big as the most horrific thing I could imagine having to endure. When you are in the middle of your own fire, it is just as important as another's. Do not ever let someone tell you that your past is insignificant. Your past is what molds you into who you are today. Your past is what gives you the hesitancy but also the courage to take certain steps in your future.

I was blessed to be born into a wonderful and loving family. Two wonderful Christian parents raised me. I was at church every time the door was open. As a family, we were involved in every church activity there was. I went to church camp during the summer and retreats during the school year. I was raised conservatively and lived in what many would call "a bubble." I honestly was not exposed to hurt, pain, or any life-altering experiences until the summer between my sophomore and junior year in high school.

I can remember to this day driving out of my driveway my sophomore year in high school with blue skies and the sun shining, thinking to myself, *Wow, I have it pretty good.* I had parents that loved me and were together. I had a boyfriend, who I thought at the time I was in love with. School was going okay. I was on the varsity tennis team playing second seat in doubles. Life was good. I did not have anything to worry about in my life. My parents provided for my brother and me. We never went without. At times I thought we were poor, but now as an adult with kids, I see just how rich we were. Not so much in money but in the family I was blessed with and the experiences I was given.

Little did I know, in the next few months a choice I had made a few months prior would begin a landslide of circumstances that would leave me ashamed, hurt, rejected, defeated, alone, and begging for someone to love me. I would be in a desperate place I had never been before. I would choose to try and fix it on my own. I would become so ashamed of the things I allowed to take place that I would begin shutting people out of my life, but more importantly, I would shut God out.

A girl with no help, hope, and future is a girl who feels an overwhelming burden of being unworthy and unloved. A woman who is so overwhelmed by the hardships of life can choose to build a wall and not let others in. In fact, for someone to get into a woman's heart, the wall must be climbed, and sometimes the wall is built too high. If anyone makes it halfway up the wall without plummeting back down, they have made it farther than most. We allow fear and a lack of trust to consume us. When someone begins to get close, we pull away.

God is alive and working in your life no matter your past, what you have done, or where you are today! Your healing, help, and hope come from Jesus!

I have watched the journey of a dear friend and have seen him transform over the years. His past, his heartache, and his struggle have allowed him to fulfill his divine purpose in life. The addiction in his life that left him thinking his life was over was the very thing that saved him. This is a post he made one Sunday after church: "Hearing Dave's sermon this morning reminded me of a time in my life when I truly believed I couldn't make it back from the place I was at. I remember looking at my mother during this rough time and saying, 'Mom, it's too late for me; I can't be saved.'"

I was not just talking about the horrible physical shape I was in from a hard lifestyle either. I felt almost certain that God had given up on me and that He had finally realized I was a lost cause. Sound dark? Trust me, it was! *But* that's not the end of the story.

Even though I had run so far in the opposite direction, God was right there with me the whole time. Just waiting *on me*. If you're in a place where you feel hopeless and forever lost, it is *not too late* for you! If you are still breathing, you still have the opportunity to have peace and live life to the fullest, through Him!

What encouragement that is! To see someone you love finally say, "God, it's *you*! It's all about *you*! Not me, not what I can do, but what *you* can do in me!" Where He takes the worst parts of us and uses the very thing that is killing us and brings us back to life! God forgives your past. There is no sin so great that God would ever abandon you. What you cannot forget, God has already forgiven. It is just us taking the first step to say, "God, here I am! Use me!" The good, the bad, and the ugly! Use it all for Your glory! We miss out on the power of God when we try to fix it ourselves instead of trusting Him.

What a miserable woman I was until I was free in Christ! It is time for you, my friend, to move into the healing that is found in Jesus Christ.

You need healing from your past. No matter the insignificance or significance of your past. Healing must take place for you to spiritually, mentally, physically, and emotionally become the person God intended you to be.

During my sophomore year in high school, I was playing tennis when my opponent served a far-angled short serve that left me sprinting onto another player's court to return the ball. All I remember was twisting my ankle, and everything went black. I woke up to severe pain shooting all through my body. I was immediately nauseous and dizzy. I was embarrassed and humiliated. I tried getting up and walking off the court on my own, but it was very apparent that I was not making it anywhere without assistance. Little did I know this was the beginning of leaning on others. I found myself becoming less helpful and more dependent on others over the next few weeks. I had sprained my ankle so badly that I was told I would have been better off breaking it. The healing process would have been much easier had I just broken my ankle. In order for me to be able to play tennis again or even walk again, I had to allow myself time to heal. I had to have help. I had to take the correct measures for my ankle to properly heal.

This is the same with our past. It is not ever a one-day fix or solution. You must allow yourself the time to heal. It may take counseling, friends, family, prayer, being alone, or a combination of them all to finally confront your past and begin to heal.

We all need help in life. Some of us are better at asking for help than others, but we all need guidance and reassurance of what we are striving for. We need the accountability that comes with help. We need someone to keep encouraging us and nudging us along on the days we are ready to give up. The accountability of someone else gives you the opportunity for a different perspective.

I went to college and received my teaching certificate. I thought I was ready and knew exactly what the classroom would be like. I had all these wonderful ideas and fun activities my students would love doing. I had the idea they would all be listening, engaged, and learning. At least I thought so. I was not prepared for what would take place in a real-world classroom. I was not prepared for the behaviors I would have to address. I was not prepared for what would take place with parents.

I needed help. I still do to this day. If we are not searching for help or better ideas, then we stay stagnant and never grow. We never learn there might be a better way to do things or an easier way to get things accomplished. Even when my limits are pushed, there are ways I can manage the stress that comes along and leaves me frazzled.

I thought I knew about raising children, relationships, true friendships, and how to be a great wife, mother, and daughter. I thought; I thought; I thought. No matter what I thought I knew or what I think I know now, I am finding it is often far from what my thoughts ever were. Sometimes my thoughts are exceeded with something much more amazing than I had imagined. More times than not, my thoughts are nowhere in the ballpark of where I thought a situation, a phase, or a season of life would be. I need help, and so do you! Help with an addiction, with relationships, with finances, parenting, or depression? Whatever it may be, do not let it take your life.

Have you ever sat and questioned if God really cares about you or questioned if there is a God? I have found myself multiple times in life asking those very questions. I could not understand why God would allow such pain and suffering or why God would allow such uncertainty in life. Why God would seem nonexistent during some of life's hardest circumstances.

Yet God reveals Himself and is there to help us when we are hurting. It takes us asking God to just help us be better and more like Him. Admitting we are trying but just cannot seem to get it right. It takes us being open to His timing and not ours. I know how frustrating it is at times to see God helping everyone else, and you still feel stuck in the same rut—dealing with the same pain and still fighting for some relief. Hold on, my friend. Hold on tight, and never let go. God will reveal Himself at just the right time with just the right thing.

We all need help spiritually as well. Even if you know God exists and never question if God cares, you need the support of other Christians. You need other Christians rallying beside you during the difficult seasons of life.

The Sunday before my divorce was finalized, I came to my church family pleading for help, requesting prayers for my kids and me. This is the letter I wrote to the congregation.

> I come asking for prayers for my kids and I as tomorrow we close a chapter in our lives. Marriage is never a clear path with a guaranteed outcome and after almost 13 years of marriage a chapter is being closed. There are many emotions right now and days that it is almost too overwhelming.
>
> I have already had my share of pain in this life but have seen God's work at hand over and over. God has redeemed every hurt and pain I have experienced thus far in life and I know He will continue to do the same. He has placed me where I needed to be, when I needed to be there on this journey of life. This is not the road I would have chosen nor the outcome I have ever wanted, and there are days it is hard to see God's hands at work when the pain is so deep. I have hope in Him and like everything else in my life we will come out much stronger and wiser.
>
> On the days when the hurt, the pain, the insecurities, the loneliness, and the self-doubt seem unbearable; please lift my kids and I up in prayer. I deal with worry, anxiety, and depression and it has held me captive many different times throughout my life. It has robbed me of precious moments I can never

get back. So, I come asking for prayers. Prayers for strength to get through the days, months, and even the years to come. Prayers for wisdom for me to be able to say and do the right things for my kids. To be God's light and keep pressing forward. Prayers for contentment so that I may focus on the important things and not dwell in the loneliness. Prayers for grace and forgiveness towards my ex as well as myself so that anger and bitterness does not chain me down. And most importantly prayers that my ex and I maintain a healthy relationship where our kids feel loved. Where they see that even in the midst of hurt and pain, good can prevail, for God's hands are always at work.

I have already been blessed beyond measure. From my parents, family, friends, and a wonderful church family- I say Thank You! I have been shown love that I could have never imagined. There are no words for the gratitude and humbleness I feel. You will never know how your love and generosity have already helped me through the hard days.

So, as our story continues to be written, please hold our hands and please lift us up in prayer.

As I look back now, I see the power in prayer. Many days I did not know how I was going to make it one more day, but I had brothers and sisters in Christ who were lifting my kids and my name up to the One Almighty. God was carrying me on those days I felt so alone and defeated, and on the days when I felt like my life was over. When I felt I had failed as a wife and as a mother. When my heart hurt so badly because my family had just become another statistic, God was there. He was always there.

The Lord created us to do life together. Choose to do life in a community of believers instead of doing it alone. No one is strong enough to do life on his or her own. We were not meant to carry life's burdens alone. Do you find yourself neck high in debt, an unhealthy relationship, overwhelmed, or shattered? Often it comes from us trying to fix one thing with another thing. We continue to add burden upon burden, because we are trying to fill a hole only God can fill.

I have always longed for love, so when a man showed interest in me, I clung to him. When happiness wavered in our relationship, we brought a child into this world. I thought a baby would make me happy. The stress of children piled on top of a marriage that struggled daily, along with a mortgage and unending bills, made life harder and more challenging. Marriage, children, and bills: these are all a part of many of our lives. I was searching for love but added burden upon burden never receiving the love I longed for.

If you feel completely alone and like there is no one on this earth who can help you and who will listen to you, do not feel alone. Someone can. His name is Jesus. You are never alone. Begin building a relationship with Him. If you already have a relationship with God, then continue talking to Him and being in His Word. He is your go-to when problems arise, when emotions run high, and when happiness occurs. He is your all-encompassing Father who is faithful until the end.

For you to move away from your past and into your future, you must have hope—hope for a future. Hope that only Jesus Christ offers and having a confidence in what is to come. If you are living in Him, your team wins. No more stress. No more burdens. You were created to make a difference—created for a purpose. If you dwell on your past, you cannot flourish in your future.

My preacher, Dave, depicted being on Jesus's team as this: "You have a DVR. You are able to record shows and games you are not at the time able to watch. Sometimes you find out the ending score before getting a chance to watch the game that you missed. When you sit down to watch the game, you know the end result. You know the final score. You do not have to stress about what is going to happen because you already know the outcome." It is the same with us. We do not know what the end result maybe, but we know God knows the end result. God sees everything before, during, and after the choices, the seasons, the tears that make us stress and carry burdens we were never intended to carry. Let God take the very things that hold you down and make you feel unworthy. Let Him take the relationships that leave you depleted. Let Him carry you through the stages of addiction. Let Him hold you during the loss of a relationship, a person, or a job. God sees what we do not see!

Do not be a prisoner of your past. Do not keep yourself locked up and behind bars because of choices, situations, or relationships that have held you captive for so many years. You must give yourself grace in the midst of heartache.

The best things are still to come because He came out of the tomb. We have hope and healing in Jesus. Stop focusing on your imperfections and start focusing on the excellence of Him. There is always hope. Everything is possible.

Scriptures to Reflect On

Forget the former things; do not dwell on the past. See, I am doing a new thing! Now it springs up; do you not perceive it? I am making a way in the wilderness and streams in the wasteland. (Isaiah 43:18–19 NIV)

Let us hold unswervingly to the hope we profess, for he who promised is faithful. (Hebrews 10:23)

Brothers and sisters, I do not consider myself yet to have taken hold of it. But one thing I do: Forgetting what is behind and straining toward what is ahead, I press on toward the goal to win the prize for which God has called me heavenward in Christ Jesus. (Philippians 3: 13–14)

He heals the brokenhearted and binds up their wounds. (Psalm 147: 3)

Even though I walk through the darkest valley, I will fear no evil, for you are with me; your rod and your staff, they comfort me. (Psalm 23:4)

May the God of hope fill you with all joy and peace as you trust in him, so that you may overflow with hope by the power of the Holy Spirit. (Romans 15:13)

Chapter 2

Words

"Sticks and stones may break my bones, but words will never hurt me." How many times have you heard this statement? I remember as a child being told by other adults this very same phrase encouraging me to just turn the other cheek when my peers said hurtful words. That is one of the most misguided statements ever. Our words are so precious, yet we allow them to roll off our tongues without a thought or care of the effects they may have on others. Words can have a more permanent effect than any broken bone ever will.

When a bone is broken, it can recover and mend. Depending on the break it may need surgery, but over time a broken bone heals. Yes, there is pain, but typically it is temporary, without lasting effects. Certain circumstances and injuries have a lasting effect, but most broken bones heal. You would never know you had the injury. The words you say to others can hurt way more than any broken bone ever will. Some words pierce straight to your heart, leaving you devastated and causing pain that may never go away. It is a pain that dictates so much of who you become. The words give you insecurities. The words make you question the things you once believed.

Think of the many different sizes of rocks. You have small pebbles all the way up to gigantic boulders. No matter if you were hit with small pebbles or gigantic boulders, it would not feel good. If you were hit by a small pebble, it would sting a little bit, but the pain would subside fairly quickly. The mark would disappear soon. If you were hit by a big rock, there would be intense pain. Marks would be made.

Pain would last for a much longer time. In some cases, the rock may leave a scar on your skin because of the force and size of the rock thrown. It is the same with your words. When you choose to throw your opinions and judgments on others, you can leave permanent scars on their souls:

- Scars to the sixteen-year-old girl whose life is unraveling and all she hears is the lady saying, "How will this affect the church?"
- Scars to the woman who is told she is not loved.
- Scars to the woman whose friend reaches out needing just one friend, one person to be there, and all she does is reject him repeatedly.
- Scars to the girl who is teased over and over about her physical appearance and is taunted by the words "you better never get fat, or I will leave you."
- Scars to the mother who constantly questions what words she has said or actions she has made toward her children, wondering about the hurt and pain it will cause them later in life.
- Scars to the woman who is made to feel stupid by others because of the way she reacts or does not react to questions being asked.

The words you speak should be used to build people up, not tear them down. Your words can lead people down a certain path—a path that is encouraging and uplifting or a path that is destructive and debilitating. Your words can cause others to start building a wall where others cannot enter. When we hear something over and over, we start to believe it. An individual's words can cause another to feel less than he or she is. Words impact our lives in unimaginable ways. Are the words you say impacting those around you in a positive way? No matter the truth of the words being spoken, those words impact our lives.

It is so important that you are not only using words to build others up but also to build yourself up. If you are not careful, you can sabotage your own image.

When my daughter hears me saying negative things about my body or sees me look in the mirror with disgust all over my face, I am setting the wrong example. When she hears my moans and groans because the clothes just do not look the same on me as they do on the model in the magazine or the mannequin in the store, and I bash my flaws, she picks up on this. I am not only feeding my mind with negative thoughts about myself, but I am teaching my daughter to perceive her body in a negative way.

My body shaming includes my freckles. It is something that is a part of me and has been all my life. Out of the mouths of babes— children tend to point out or questions things. As all my jobs since high school have involved kids, it did not take long before kids began asking me what the brown dots on my body were. I was already self-conscious of my freckles and became even more so as they were pointed out. I have learned over the years to embrace my freckles and joke that if only all my freckles would connect, I would have one amazing tan.

The older I get, the more I am making comments about my wrinkles and how my body is changing. I went to bed one night, and the next morning there was a wrinkle under my chin. What in the world? You literally have four years or so that is your prime, and then everything just goes south from there. Seriously, at least for me! How in the world is that fair? Those wrinkles we wish would go away or pray would never show up show our life. Wrinkles depict the amount of sun and tanning our bodies have seen over the years. Wrinkles also depict the life we have been dealt—the long nights we have stayed awake crying, the nights and days left worrying over circumstances out of our control, and the fears we carry of making yet another mistake in our lives or our families' lives. Our wrinkles are a testament that we are getting older but also signify the wisdom we have acquired over the years. Each wrinkle has a story.

I am also notorious for complaining about having a muffin top when I wear my jeans. I have never and will never have a six-pack. I like my sodas and food just a little too well. I sure like to gripe about my roll hanging over my pants or the back fat my bra creates, but I do not have a strong enough desire to change my eating habits in order to enhance my appearance. We need to embrace our flaws. Embrace the things we dislike about ourselves. We must build up our daughters, as well as ourselves, at home. We must prepare them with strength and confidence to face the world outside the walls of our homes!

If we do not teach our daughters to have confidence and give them the tools to look at themselves through Christ's eyes, this world will tear them apart with its harsh criticism and cruel taunts. I am not saying if you have it, flaunt it. There is a modest way in which to teach our girls how to love and respect their bodies. There will be negativity in life. I believe it is human nature to not be happy with something about yourself or desire for a part of yourself to be better. You must intentionally give your attention to the things you like about your body rather than focus on the things you do not like. We have all heard this saying: "If you cannot say anything nice, then do not say anything at all." We should not only be putting that into practice when we speak to others but also when we speak to ourselves. When you look in the mirror, tell yourself you are beautiful. You have a purpose. You are loved. Say this every day, every time you see your reflection. You may not believe it now, but keep saying it, and you will begin to believe it. Do not let Satan come in and tell you lies. When life leaves you feeling defeated, do not fill your head with negativity.

It was not until the past couple of years that I have started asking myself, "How am I showing Christ through my actions and my words to those who have hurt me the most?" or "How am I being Christ-like when all I do is bash those who have wronged me or my family?" I know that many days I am throwing rocks. Big rocks, to hurt people instead of building them up. It does not even have to be words said to the person himself or herself but to others. The way you talk about someone to another can have the exact effects as if you were saying it to the person's face.

After going out with my girlfriends one night, I came home feeling extremely anxious and emotional. The next morning, I sent a text to each of my friends who were with me the night before.

> I send this today asking for accountability. The struggle is very deep, and I know it plays a big part in my anxiety. You girls know more than anyone about the pain and hurt I endured in my marriage. I know I am not innocent in our problems. I bash him and run his name through the mud with you girls. Yes, it feels good at the time and maybe to an extent it is a part of healing, but I need to rein it in and stop. I am tired of saying his name every time we are together, although it is hard because for fifteen years it has been his name. So, I am pleading that you rein me in on the days I want to bash him. For me to fully heal and to move on, I have to give him grace. For me, I need to show it not just in everyone else's eyes but your eyes as well. I cannot have nights like last night where I cry myself to sleep with guilt for the way I speak and act toward him. Where my feelings at the time feel justified, it is not the person I want to be. I know you probably think I am crazy. I question that myself sometimes. Lol. But I have to do this for me. I love you all deeply and I know this may seem crazy for me to ask of you, but I need the accountability. I need it shut down when I do not have the will power to shut it down myself. I need your help! Thank you from the bottom of my heart.

I felt so much justification in anything I said about my ex. To the world I did have the justification, but I do not want to be of this world. I want to be of God. In order to be of God, I must control my anger on social media. I must not drag his name through the mud or display every fault he had. I must not bash his name when others are around. It is so easy for me to see the fault of his but not see the faults of my own. Jesus said in Mathew 7:5: "You hypocrite, first take the plank out of your own eye, and then you will see clearly to remove the speck from your brother's eye." I upset myself when I speak negatively about the problems of my relationship. Speaking negatively only stirs the emotions within me and sends me on an emotional roller coaster going faster than I want it to and shaking me all up.

It takes a lot of restraint to not point out the faults of others. You want everyone to know the hurt they have caused. The pain you have endured. The ridicule you have taken. The tears you have shed. The screams you have cried. The fears you have hidden. The loneliness you have felt.

It is not just the words we say that leave a person's soul broken and lost, but it can also be in the words we do not say. I have lived with guilt for many years because of words I never said. As a young adult, I was married and had my own children when an ex-boyfriend moved back to our hometown. He reached out to me some, and I would push him away. I would make excuses as to why I could not talk or be at certain events he was going to be at. Then life really hit him hard, and his world turned upside down. When he needed a friend, I still pushed him away. The pain I endured in high school kept me from being a friend.

He had been staying at my mom's house through all his turmoil, but one night he never showed up at her house. He had left town. The next day we found out he had taken one of many pills during the hours of the night, and he was found the next day unresponsive.

I still have dreams. I still ask the "what ifs." If I had just put my selfishness to the side, forgotten about the hurt and pain he caused, and taken time to just be a friend. Nothing more than just a friend who could listen, who could rally alongside him and let him know he was not alone in this life. It becomes so easy to stay fixed on ourselves and our own emotions and what someone did to us rather than to just put our differences aside and love one another.

I have watched a sweet girl in my hometown grow into a beautiful young lady. When I look at her and listen to her hurt, struggles, and self-esteem, I see myself in her. I feel for her because I once was a girl with no confidence and settling for things I really did not want because I felt that was all I was worthy of. I gave my opinions and told her exactly how I thought her life would turn out if she did not make changes. I supported her, but I talked until I was blue in the face spewing my opinions on her. I did not want her to experience the same kind of hurt I had experienced in life. I did not want her to make the same mistakes I had made in my own life. I told her what she deserved in life and what a beautiful woman she was. In my mind I was showing love. I only wanted what was best for her, but instead I hurt her. I did not speak love to her. I spoke demands.

When someone is broken and hurting, he or she does not need you to add to the brokenness with your words. You see the person is already devastated, is already in pain, and is already suffering. The individual does not need to hear that he or she is wrong. The person does not need you telling him or her that he or she is lost. The person knows just how lost he or she already is. The sufferer needs love and to be spoken to in love. If we are not careful, the words we think we speak in love are the actual words that drive that person further down the road of insecurities, heartbreak, and depression.

I struggle many days and mess up on more days than I would like to admit in the words I say to others. I am not good with my words. I tend to say the wrong thing, or the words come out a different way than what I am thinking in my head. I also get lost at times in my own selfishness and craziness of life. It is not until the person walks away or sometimes the next day that I realize what I should have said. We are human, and it is so easy to lash out and give our own opinion. Our words may have no significance to some, but to others our words may be the very thing that brings a smile to their day or tears to them at night. What scars are you leaving them with?

Think of how many times you have been hurt by flying rocks (words) by others—even by Christians? How do you use your words? Are you using words to create pathways to God and to build them up? Or are you using your words to damage and destroy the essence of their being? What good are we accomplishing by throwing rocks at one another?

I often find myself biting my tongue because somebody will say something that crawls all over me. I want to be a smart aleck. I want to say something hurtful. Sometimes I have every justification to make the comment I am thinking. It is in those moments that I can choose to restrain from saying the words I feel I need to say and choose to show Christ instead. Some people are much easier to refrain from speaking to. Then there are others or situations where it takes every ounce of your being to not say something. It is hard to not react when you feel you have every right to react.

Words do not just affect you in the moment; they leave you with wounds that sometimes are left open to fester and never heal. Words can pierce through everything you are. Once you hear something enough times, you start to believe it. The words pierce through your soul, leaving you feeling insignificant and belittled.

Did you ever have that one teacher who said such hateful words? The teacher who talked in such a hateful tone? Due to that one teacher or that one class, you began to dislike school or even hate school. That one year or bad semester ruined the rest of your school career. We let one bad apple ruin what we think or how we perceive things. Actually, you had way more great teachers than bad teachers. You just let the bad outweigh the good.

When you choose to let those words or phrases that have been said to you fester, you become bitter and resentful. You become defensive, and at some point, your words are shooting out the same pain your soul has agonized over. I know it is not easy. I get it. I have fought my entire life to not let the words of others hurt me so much. The hurtful words that have been spoken to me in my past have consumed me at times. Those words have left me in disbelief at times, wondering how in the world someone who loved me would say or do such things. Those words spoken to me have also left me ready to fight. Ready to throw the biggest rock I can find—the one that will cut right into their souls as they did mine.

What is being accomplished by doing that? Nothing. In the moment or for days afterward I may get satisfaction from the words I said. Maybe the words I said needed to be said, but they did not need to be said in a tone that was hurtful.

I have attended some conferences discussing the emphasis of how you say a word. The way we say even one word can change the way a sentence is taken. The tone in our voice changes everything we mean. I can make a statement saying, "I said you might consider waiting." It is just a simple statement, but when I put emphasis on different words, it changes what I am saying. Say the sentence again putting emphasis on the italicized words. "*I* said you might consider waiting." When you put emphasis on the word *I*, you are saying it was your idea. "I *said* you might consider waiting." When you put emphasis on the word *said*, you are questioning if they understand you. "I said *you* might consider waiting." When you put emphasis on the word *you*, it means no other person but the one you are talking to. "I said you *might* consider waiting." When you put emphasis on the word *might*, you are saying it is a possibility. "I said you might *consider* waiting." When you put emphasis on the word *consider*, you are saying they should think about it or it is a good idea. "I said you might consider *waiting*." When you put emphasis on the word *waiting*, you mean nothing else. We let emotions speak our words.

I have spent so many years feeling like I was not very smart. I would be asked a question, and when an immediate response was not given, I would be left feeling stupid. It is a processing thing for me. I must repeat it in my head sometimes. Even when I am not repeating what was just asked in my head, many times I am pondering over the questions and the words. I am thinking what my answer should be, and at times, I have a hard time with a response. I am not good with my words when an instant response is needed. It is something I have always struggled with.

We all have moments and things we would have done or said differently. Just because your response is not as quick or as good as the one asking does not mean your thoughts or your words are less important. Do not allow others' perceptions of you to dwindle your worth. Being slow to answer is not a bad thing, In James 1:19, James tells us we should be slow to speak.

Words are what brought this world into existence. Words are what will lead us to our death. They cause our disagreements, our fights, and our wars. We need our hearts changed. We need our hearts transformed. Only through the Word of God are we able to speak words of kindness to others.

Scriptures to Reflect On

You hypocrite, first take the plank out of your own eye, and then you will see clearly to remove the speck from your brother's eye. (Mathew 7:5)

My dear brothers and sisters, take note of this: Everyone should be quick to listen, slow to speak and slow to become angry, because human anger does not produce the righteousness that God desires. (James 1:19–20)

Let your conversation be always full of grace, seasoned with salt, so that you may know how to answer everyone. (Colossians 4:6)

Do not let any wholesome talk come out of your mouths, but only what is helpful for building others up according to their needs, that it may benefit those who listen. (Ephesians 4:29)

Sin is not ended by multiplying words, but the prudent hold their tongues. (Proverbs 10:19)

The soothing tongue is a tree of life, but a perverse tongue crushes the spirit. (Proverbs 15:4)

The heart of the righteous weighs its answers, but the mouth of the wicked gushes evil. (Proverbs 15:28)

What goes into someone's mouth does not defile them, but what comes out of their mouth, that is what defiles them. (Matthew 15:11)

Those who guard their mouths and tongues keep themselves from calamity. (Proverbs 21:23)

Set a guard over my mouth, Lord; keep watch over the door of my lips. (Psalm 141:3)

The words of the reckless pierce like swords, but the tongue of the wise brings healing. (Proverbs 12:18)

A gentle answer turns away wrath, but a harsh word stirs up anger. The tongue of the wise adorns knowledge, but the mouth of the fool gushes folly. (Proverbs 15:1–2)

Chapter 3

Worldly Satisfaction

I can remember as a little girl daydreaming about what my future would look like. I played the games where you wrote the names of boys you like, wrote different numbers for how many kids you would have, wrote the places of where you would live, wrote the pets you would have, and wrote really anything else your heart desired. With a song or a folded piece of paper, which we called a fortune-teller, you would determine what your future held. If only it were that simple, and life would just fall into place the way we had mapped it out on paper.

I dreamed of the happiness life would bring, the joys life had to give, and the love that would await me. Little did I know, as a child, that life is often filled with more hurt than joy. My happiness in life would be further away and more in between than I ever wished for. My struggles in life would be more than I felt I could bear at times. My relationships would bring me to my breaking point but would also be my saving grace. I would question God. I would not understand certain things that would happen and why they had to take place. I would see how easy it was for some to hurt me with no care in the world and how others would stand beside me until the bitter end no matter what circumstances arose. Life would be completely different than I ever dreamed.

My life would begin unraveling. My dreams, the path I would choose to take, and the curveballs life would bring would leave me nowhere near the dreams I had mapped out on that piece of paper.

I never felt neglected, not loved, or unlovable as a child. I was encouraged and spoken to in a positive way. Yet I struggled with my self-esteem. As I entered high school, my self-esteem was not great, and it declined through the years. I yearned to be popular and for my peers to want me around. I wanted acceptance for how I looked and for who I was.

I did not get attention from boys like my peers were getting. This made me question what was wrong with me. In my eyes, when I looked in the mirror, I did not see beauty. I saw a girl who longed to fit in—a girl with stringy brown hair who looked like a twig. I was flat in the chest and flat in the butt. I desperately wanted curves. I wanted to be in style with my clothing, and I wanted to know how to do my makeup like I saw so many of my other friends wearing.

I remember being teased about my ears numerous times in school, but the incident that has kept my ears covered until this very day was a boy at Six Flags who made one gesture and said one word. After sitting on the Texas Giant rollercoaster and pulling the bar to my lap, a boy I did not know thumped my ears and called me "Dumbo." That scarred me for life. To this very day if my hair is pulled up or back, my hair has to cover my ears, or I wear a headband that lies over my ears. It is silly, but no matter how many times I have tried to let my ears show, I always go back to covering them up. I am consumed with worry about what others will think about how I look.

When a boy noticed me and I was given the attention I was longing for, lines were crossed, and morals went to the side. I did things I said I would never do. It was not an immediate thing that took place in my relationship, but it was something I allowed when I sensed things were headed south. I was going to hang on to the attention I was receiving, no matter the cost. I had no idea of what the "cost" would be. My innocence was taken away. The purity and the wholeness of my mind and body had no significance anymore. The feelings of being wanted and loved held me clinging to the person who would do just that.

Our world and our culture have become so accustomed to our outward appearances that we hardly ever look at what is on the inside of a person. We do not look at the how and what of a person's makeup. How often do we judge people just by the clothes they wear, the way they look on one particular day or week, or by the things that come out of their mouths? I am guilty of it. I am aware of it and try my best to be self-conscious about it, but I still find myself on many days judging people because of what they wear or say or how they sound.

Social media and technology play a big part in our self-esteem. We are all very aware of that. There are so many good things social media and technology provide us as a society, but there are also so many things that derail the mind-set, the courage, the self-esteem, and the well-being of so many young lives. I, myself, am not big on all the social media sites. I learn more from my kids about what the new apps or games are. What the "in" thing is. My kids do not understand why, at the ages of ten and twelve, they cannot have social media accounts. There is enough hurt and hatred at school. My kids do not need another avenue to be hurt and to see the skewed views of the world in which we live.

I know the things girls and young women see through TV, movies, and social media that play into them believing certain stereotypes about themselves. We as parents, as friends, as family, as teachers, and as a society must let these girls and young women know that there is much more to life than how we appear on the outside. You may have some rocking hot body as a young girl or woman, and if you can keep that figure for the rest of your life, kudos to you. As for the rest of us, whether we thought we were pretty in high school and had the best body ever or we hated what we saw in the mirror, we do not resemble now what we did then. Our bodies change. Life and time take hold of us, and we change.

Sometimes the change is for the better. You choose to look at your outward appearance, and you choose to embrace the body God gave you. When you choose to accept the changes of your body, you are just signifying the life you have endured thus far and how your body has coped with the stress of life.

Sometimes the change is for the worse. We allow our outward appearance to dictate our happiness. We do not even like ourselves, so how in the world would anyone else ever like us? We either have positive self-esteem with an attitude of "I can wear it and rock it," or we are so insecure and worried about how others will think of us and what they might say.

I have heard people say it's all about size, but I have seen the tiniest of girls and women wear baggie clothes and be completely insecure and with no self-esteem. I see plus-size girls and women who have the best self-esteem and are the happiest of people. I have heard people say it all depends on your outward appearance. If you look nice and put together, you will be more confident. If you do not look put together, then you have insecurities and low self-esteem. It does not matter if you have the nicest clothes or are wearing sweats, if your hair is down or up, or if you have makeup on or not. It comes down to us being comfortable in our own bodies—whatever our shape, size, or color. We were created for a purpose. We were created just as God wanted. Many of us question why God made us the way He did or why God did not make us a certain way. Do not allow this world to question those things. This world needs you and your exact beauty! You bring something special to this world! Be true to who you are, and do not change for others' approval.

Having a daughter has challenged me to watch what I say about myself and even others, especially when she is around. I have caught myself looking in the mirror on many occasions saying, "Ugh. So gross. That's nasty looking. Whew, I need to lose weight. Disgusting. Gag, that makes me want to throw up."

I thrive on the things people say to me. My love language is affirmations. When someone tells me that my outfit is cute or that I look pretty, my self-esteem skyrockets. When anyone affirms the way I look or something I am doing, that makes me feel the most loved. When days go by and no comments are made, I start to question what is wrong with me. I question myself asking if I should not wear a certain outfit again. I wonder what I need to do to my outward appearance so that others will notice. I question if what I am doing is not really a big deal or if I should be doing something else.

Just as the Bible says in Mathew 6:1, there are good deeds we should do in private with no expectation of being affirmed. Buying someone's meal or groceries, helping a single mom with her children for the night so she can have some peace and quiet, or whatever it may be, these are things I do not do for affirmation. I do those things to simply show Christ Jesus and to give to others, expecting nothing in return.

I love fashion. I may not be a fashionista, but one of my weaknesses is buying clothes and shoes. Some of my shopping sprees derive from a lack of compliments and self-esteem. It is sad. What kind of example am I setting for my daughter? What perceptions am I allowing to cross her mind about how she should look at her own body? I do not want my daughter or any girl to ever think that happiness comes from the way you perceive yourself naked in front of the mirror or by the clothes you wear. Your happiness comes from within your heart and soul.

It does the heart and soul good to get dressed up, put makeup on, and have hair fixed, but at the end of the day our physical appearance should not be the thing that reigns over our self-esteem. Not only does our body image affect our self-esteem, but our social experiences and our performance in whatever it is we are doing affects our self-esteem as well. Experiences from school, home, work, or even church can build us or break us. The way we perform in our jobs, sports, academics, or whatever we are striving for in life influences our self-esteem. At the age of thirty-five, I still struggle at times with my self-esteem. It is not anywhere near the degree it once was, but it's an insecurity that if I am not careful can send me into a downward spiral. I am learning to embrace my weight being the most it ever has been and say it is okay. I am happy, and I finally love myself.

Let me take you back to my first relationship where I saw an entirely new me, and where I let my emotions take control of my morals. Eight months after we started dating, I was left completely devastated. My boyfriend broke up with me. He was my first boyfriend and my first love, or so I thought. It wouldn't be until almost twenty years later that I would realize what love is. I thought my life was falling apart. I cried for two days straight. I had not only lost a relationship, but I had lost a part of me. I wallowed in my despair. I lost something God intended to be special. I gave it away with no thought at all. The beauty and meaningfulness between a man and a woman as they become one was stripped away from me. It was done by my choice, and I could not change that.

I admire young girls who make their list of must-haves for their husbands-to-be. I am not talking about the fortune-teller paper. I am talking about a list of characteristics, morals, and beliefs that she desires and expects of a husband. I have watched as girls wait until they are in college to date, and their dates are minimal. They stick to their list. They do not sway in the qualities they have for the man they want to spend the rest of their lives with. To have that determination and willpower to stick with what you believe in at such a young age deserves much recognition. I had my own list as well with characteristics, morals, and beliefs, but I let fear, loneliness, and desire take hold. I compromised what I believed for worldly satisfaction. I gave no consideration to the consequences that would follow or how my life would become so much harder. My innocence was gone. Things would be more complex from here on.

I trusted many adults in my life. I began reaching out to a man I trusted and looked up to about my relationship with my ex-boyfriend. I confided in him about my relations with my ex-boyfriend. I trusted him. I opened up to him about my sins. I confessed that my beliefs and morals were compromised for personal desires and attention. He gave me advice and listened to me. I spent many days with his family.

School was out, and I was enjoying the summer. If I was not doing church or youth group activities, then I was babysitting. I had a handful of families I would babysit for. I not only babysat for many of these families, but I spent lots of time just hanging out and building relationships with them.

One evening as I left from babysitting, a line was crossed. Not knowing or understanding what had just happened, I got into my vehicle and went straight home. I said nothing to my parents; I said not a word to anyone. In my sixteen-year-old mind, I did not know how to process what had just happened. So, not knowing or understanding what was taking place, I went back to his house the next morning to babysit.

When I got there, inappropriate actions occurred, and trust was broken. Once I got back home, I took the longest shower I had ever taken in my life, sobbing for what I had allowed to take place. I felt filthy. I was a horrible person. I allowed an act to happen that never should have taken place. As guilt consumed me, I said nothing to anyone—not even my best friend. It was a secret I would carry for the next six months. Those next months ate me alive.

A few weeks passed after that morning. I remember the day like it was yesterday. It was a sweltering summer day in July. I had been swimming all day with a little girl I babysat. We took a small nap break and returned for more fun. When we returned to the pool where her mom and sister were, I was approached by others telling me my mom was looking for me. My cell phone was dead. I tried using someone else's phone to call my mom, but the line was busy. When I was not able to reach her, the lady I was babysitting for decided to follow me to my mom's workplace to find out what she wanted before heading back to the lady's house.

As I walked into my mom's workplace I saw her standing behind the counter with our preacher and another man. As our eyes met, she rushed down the aisle to tell me that my dad and brother had been in an accident. My brother had broken his arm, and they were not sure how my dad was.

My dad and brother were on their way back from visiting my grandmother when a young man swerved off the road. When he overcorrected, he struck the truck in which my dad and brother were traveling.

My mom and I had to get to where they were taking my dad and brother. I was in my bathing suit, so my mom asked the other man who was there with the preacher to take me home so I could change, and we would meet back at her workplace. I became hysterical. I wanted to drive myself home. I tried reassuring everyone I was fine to drive. Little did they know I was not hysterical because of the wreck. I was hysterical because I was being forced to get in a vehicle with the man who broke my trust. They took my keys from me and made me get into his truck. As we drove to my house, we sat in silence. He at one point put his hand on mine. As soon as he touched my skin, I felt sick. My skin crawled. I quickly pulled my hand away. As we drove up to my house, I realized I had no way to get into the house. My keys were taken away. So, we had to take the screen off a window, and I had to crawl through the window with him pushing me through it. When you have been taken advantage of—when trust has been broken—the slightest touch can send all kinds of emotions running through your body. I was never so thankful to get back to my mom that day. I was filled with brokenness and was experiencing so many emotions.

Our preacher drove my mom and me to where my dad and brother were supposed to be. We had sixty miles to drive. My preacher drove ninety miles an hour, but it felt as though it took an eternity to get there. It was the longest drive of my life. We walked into the hospital and were immediately directed to a waiting room. I do not remember if it was a private area or what, but we were the only ones there. All I can remember is that somebody came out and said my mom's name. She stood up, and they explained to her that they had taken my brother to the nearest clinic. My brother's arm was injured, and my dad's critical injuries were fatal. I will never forget the gut-wrenching scream my mom made and the tears that poured down her cheeks.

All that resonated with me was *critical*. That was what I heard. It was not until my mom looked into my eyes and said, "your dad is gone" that I realized what had been said. I did not cry. I remember my heart pounding. It was as if I knew something was wrong, but my brain could not process what was being said. I stood there as my mom had to make the hardest phone call ever. She had to tell my dad's parents and her own what had happened. With my mom and I walking out with our arms wrapped around one another, we got in our van. We had to be driven another hour to where my brother was.

Once we got in the van, everything resonated, and the floodgates opened. As we drove to get my brother, my mom consoled me. I could not imagine my life without my dad. I was already playing in my mind all the moments my dad would not be there for. The moments we would not get to experience together.

When we got to the small-town clinic my brother was at, I was told to go into the room with him while my mom went somewhere else. As I walked into the room, the nurses were still pulling glass from my brother's arm. I stood there with him while they finished getting the glass out and stitching him up. I remember sitting there stroking his hair and thanking God that he was okay. My brother asked many times how our dad was. It was so hard to stay strong. I fought to hold back tears as I explained to him that our mom was finding out the details.

Once my brother was all stitched and bandaged up, we got into the van to head back home. It was then that my brother asked my mom about my dad, and she told him. That sunny July day forever changed my life. Within a few weeks, my whole world had crumbled. Although the sky was shining brightly that day, a huge storm had rolled in, and my life would never be the same again.

The trip home seemed to crawl by. As we pulled onto the street where we lived, cars were all down our road and in our driveway. Friends and family were already there. People met us in the driveway. Our house was full of friends who had already stocked our fridge and countertops with food. The following days are a fog. I remember not being able to eat or sleep. During the wee hours of the night, my mom and I would get up and eat a bowl of cereal alone in the quietness of the night.

I am forever grateful for the love and support that was shown to our family that day and in the days, weeks, and months to come. I truly do not understand how people get through tragedies without a church family. It was our church family who carried my mom through her hardest days. Our church family helped my mom raise her two children into the individuals they are today.

As the days turned into weeks, the guilt began to really sink in. I believed in my mind that God had taken my dad because of choices I had made. God was punishing me. I had the guilt of what my dad was driving when they were in the wreck. You see, I had turned sixteen the winter before. I was given my grandparents' '84 cracker-box delivery truck, which we named the Smurf. The Smurf was not cool! I was mortified to drive it! My dad, being the loving dad he was, let me drive his truck, which was so much cooler. The Smurf had no airbags. When the wreck happened, there was no protection whatsoever. It was metal and glass going everywhere. I told myself that if he had just been in his truck, he would have survived. If I had just not been so embarrassed of material things, he might still be alive.

I spent a lot of time at home watching my brother while my mom worked, or I was babysitting for other families. I was very emotional, and my mom could see I was struggling. She took me to the doctor, where they put me on antidepressants. We also started seeing a counselor. We would go individually and as a family. I went weekly while my mom and brother went every other week.

Life for me had become so dark. I was in pain and carried guilt no one knew about. I was grieving for the things my dad would not be present for. He would not be there to see me graduate from high school or from college. He would not be there to help me through my struggles and to rejoice in my successes. Who would walk me down the aisle when I got married? He would never hold his grandchildren. I would never again have the love only a father can provide. I lost a part of me. The love and security that once made me whole was gone. I never felt scared when growing up. Yes, I feared the dark, bugs, and thunderstorms, but I had no fears about life. For the first time in my life, I felt fear—fear for what was to come and how I would ever survive.

I have expressed my guilt about my dad not having his truck and being in what was supposed to be my truck when the accident happened. If my dad had his truck, there were airbags. And because there were airbags, maybe he would have survived. I was selfish. I wanted to be liked by my peers and fit in, and I allowed my perception of me to complain and whine enough so that my dad agreed to switch vehicles with me.

What if I had not been so selfish? What if I had just been content with driving the Smurf? The "what-ifs" do not change anything, yet we torment ourselves with how we could or would have done something differently. We eat our lives away asking those questions. We place blame on others or ourselves where blame should not be placed.

Within a few weeks of one another, my life was turned upside down in multiple ways. Fear became a force to reckon with as well as guilt. I did not understand why or what was going on. One choice, one action, one word can change the trajectory of our lives. The choices I had made in the past six months were heading me down a path I never saw coming—a path with loneliness, depression, anxiety, worthlessness, and fear. I would say I was leaning on God; I was giving Him my life, but I was controlling everything. I took the reins myself, and I made the choices that would benefit me or help me get to where I thought I needed to be. I told myself that I got myself to this point, so I could get myself out. I did not need help—not from friends and, for sure, not from God.

Scriptures to Reflect On

My flesh and my heart may fail, but God is the strength of my heart and my portion forever. (Psalm 73:26)

When tempted, no one should say, "God is tempting me." For God cannot be tempted by evil, nor does he tempt anyone; but each person is tempted when they are dragged away by their own evil desire and enticed. Then, after desire has conceived, it gives birth to sin; and sin, when it is full-grown, gives birth to death. (James 1:13–15)

For the grace of God has appeared that offers salvation to all people. It teaches us to say "No" to ungodliness and worldly passions, and to live self controlled, upright and godly lives in this present age. (Titus 2:11–12)

Do not conform to the pattern of this world, but be transformed by the renewing of your mind. Then you will be able to test and approve what God's will is— his good, pleasing and perfect will. (Romans 12:2)

Chapter 4

Made My Bed

D o you find yourself reflecting on the decisions you have made in your life that leave you feeling as though you are stuck? You become stuck in your thinking, in your actions, in fear, in your circumstances, and in your past. It comes from the choices we have made. I forever felt as though I was stuck; I could not change anything because this is where my choices in life had led me.

As the one adult male I had confided in turned my whole world upside down, I finally said something six months later to a lady for whom I babysat. I considered her to be my second mom. I spent hours every day at her house hanging out with her and her kids. I spent more time at her home than I did at my own home. A few days after confiding in her, she reached out, persuading me to let someone else know. What I had told her had been weighing heavily on her heart. Her concern was not only for me but for others too. What if this had happened to other girls, and they were being silent just as I was? After many conversations between us, I decided to tell someone else.

She and I met with my preacher one afternoon. After meeting with my preacher, it was decided we would tell my mom that evening. Telling my mom was one of the hardest things I have ever had to do. I remember sitting in a room full of our elders and their wives as well as our preacher and his wife. The only words I remember from that evening were, "How will this affect the church?"

I now know the words were not meant to hurt. I honestly do not think the words even resonated with the one who said them or how those very words could be taken. But for a girl who was carrying so much guilt and depression, those words cut straight through my heart. All I could think was how everyone was worried about how this would look and how it would affect the church. Nobody was taking into account that there was a sixteen-year-old girl who should have never been placed in a situation where she felt uncomfortable and where lines were crossed. I shut down even more after that night. I crawled deeper into my shell and built my wall even higher.

I do not remember my junior year. It is a blur. I had come to the point of being suicidal. I never had the courage to ever end my life, but it crossed my mind many times. I remember pouring a whole bottle of pills out on the kitchen counter crying out to God, asking, *Why me? Why my dad?* I sat on the floor with my head between my legs praying God would just take me—wishing God would somehow end my life because I was too chicken to do it myself. At this point I became good at hiding the pain inside and the loneliness I felt.

My self-esteem had hit rock bottom. I thought very little of myself. I doubted who I even was. I longed for male attention, and it did not matter whom it was from. I just needed somebody to look at me and think I was worth their time, effort, and love.

As a teenager, you think you know what love is. You think that you know all about life and that your parents know absolutely nothing. Times have changed since your parents were your age, and they have … This world has changed since they were teenagers. The same situations, the same feelings, and the same insecurities still exist; it is all just more substantial than it was then. Everything is more extreme and more intense. It is even worse for our own children today. As a sixteen-year-old girl, I had already endured hardships that I never thought would happen to me. This was not what I dreamed of. Somehow and some way, though, I was determined to find love. I was going to feel loved.

I managed to find some happiness going into my senior year. I was excited about it being my last year of high school, as any senior is. I had become a student trainer because of my ankle injury, which left me scared to get back on the court. In February of my senior year, I started dating a guy that was a sophomore. Yes, I robbed the cradle. I was so happy to have a male in my life. I was receiving the attention I had so longed for. I had found "love" again.

When I went off to college, we continued dating. We did the whole long-distance thing for two years. We never argued much and had a great relationship. Since we did not see each other much, when we did, we were just happy to finally be together. As he became a senior in high school and I a sophomore in college, I convinced him one night over the phone he needed to marry me. There was no proposal; there was no special moment. I went to the mall by myself and bought my own wedding ring. I justified buying my own ring by using the money I had received from my dad when he passed away. I told myself this was how my dad would be a part of our marriage. I asked him to marry me because I was so afraid that if we broke up—if he left me—no one would ever want to be with me. I would never have another boyfriend. I would always be alone. I so desperately wanted and needed to be loved, and this was the only way I could control that.

We married that summer and moved to start and finish college together. Our marriage was good for the first few years. It was not until we moved back to our hometown that our relationship started to take some hard hits. We were so young, and his friends were all single and enjoying the college life. He was married and now had a baby as well. He had gone from living with his parents to living with his wife. He never got the time to just enjoy life. To just grow and discover who he was. The partying life never appealed to me in college, and I lived for every other weekend to see him. I was in bed most nights by ten. Pretty sad, huh? And it was all for a guy. I was so desperate to keep my relationship that I did not enjoy the college years I had. I did not ever allow myself to discover the person I was. I needed love from someone else. I needed someone else to complete me. What I really needed was to love myself. But that would not come for many years and after lots of heartbreak.

As time went on, we fell into a cycle. We would be good for a month or so, and then everything would fall to shambles for the next few months. Argument after argument and fight after fight followed until one of us would finally give in, and the cycle would begin again.

We married so early in life that neither one of us had a clue about what love or life was all about. We had no clue who we were. I had in mind how I wanted our family to look and how I wanted people to perceive us. Many Saturday nights—well, actually Sunday mornings—he would come home in the wee hours. I literally made myself sick wondering where he was. I played every scenario I could ever think of but always going back to the scenario of him in a ditch dead somewhere. With two babies, getting in the car and going to look for him was not something I could do. I would try to go to sleep but would just toss and turn and stare at the clock until he would come home. We would then stand in the kitchen for hours arguing and getting nothing accomplished. It was the same fight, just another night. With only a few hours of sleep, I would get the kids and myself ready for church. With a smile on my face, I would sit in a pew fighting back tears. I became so good at "playing church."

How many of us become good at playing church? We walk into a church—the one place we should be able to let our guard down, the one place we should not feel as though we have to fake it, and the one place we should feel loved and not judged. Yet I walked into a roomful of people and sat there with shame, fear, and pain. I never reached out. I never asked for help. I just held it all in and tried for years and years to fix it myself. I wanted my marriage, my husband, and my family to be perfect. I looked at people in church—coworkers and people in our community—thinking their lives, their marriages, and their families were perfect. My life, my marriage, and my family were nowhere near perfect.

It's funny how we sit in church and keep it all together until we get home, and the tears begin to pour out. The pain cuts deep, and the loneliness sets in. We come to church to be filled. We come to church to be refueled and to get that boost of hope and encouragement to keep us going. We come to church for fellowship. In actuality we come with a fake smile and fighting back tears acting like everything in life is perfect.

What is our answer when someone asks how we are doing? It is typically "good" or "fine." A lot of times that is far from anything we feel. Instead of reaching out to others, we sit among others, feeling alone. We go home and drown ourselves in our sorrows.

The way we help others is by being vulnerable ourselves. We must share our hurts, our disappointments, and our struggles. We do not have to share the details, but we do need to share our stories. I am not alone, and neither are you. There are many people in this world who are going through or have gone through situations very similar to yours. God did not put us on this earth to do life alone. We are meant to do life together. That means being open to our good and bad as well as others' good and bad.

The older I became, the more my anxiety grew if someone was not where they were supposed to be, when they said they would be there. I knew it all stemmed from my dad's accident, and it was something that caused a wedge in our marriage. He thought I was trying to be his mother, and all I wanted was to know he was alive. Many other issues caused a wedge in our relationship. Lots of hurtful words and actions were said and done by both of us. We split up after eight years of marriage and filed for divorce.

With everything that went on between the two of us, I became bitter. Bitter toward him for treating me the way he did and bitter at friends because of how perfect their families seemed compared to mine. I even at times became bitter toward my mom because she did not understand the very few things I would talk to her about. Yet how could I be so bitter toward all these people when they had no clue about the inward struggles and feelings I dealt with daily.

Living alone for the first time in my life without having a roommate or a spouse, I learned some things about myself. One thing I discovered was that I did not need someone with me twenty-four seven. I was very capable of doing many things on my own. It was challenging to mow two acres with toddlers at home. It was challenging meeting the needs of two different toddlers and at times not wanting to pull out my hair. I managed though, and I began to build a little bit of confidence in myself. I began to realize how strong a woman I was physically and emotionally. With the help of YouTube, I was able to fix things I would have asked a man to do.

At that time I began to learn what falling to your knees in prayer was all about, and I desired for more of a relationship with God. I still, though, longed for companionship. I did not want to do this thing called life alone. I began seeing a counselor to help navigate my thoughts and emotions.

After a month or so of being separated, we decided to work things out. We stayed separated and worked on our relationship. He did not immediately move home. He still lived away, and we began going to counseling together.

I pleaded for us to not get a divorce. I did not want "us" to end. This was not where I wanted my life to be. We tried to make our marriage and our family work, and after six months of living apart he moved back home. There were happy moments that I will forever cherish. I held on to those very moments on the many days we did not see eye to eye. But eventually the same issues arose, and the cycles began again.

I knew where our mistakes were. I was not happy, and neither was he. That was very apparent. I felt like I tried and tried. I was not trying to start arguments. I was not trying to tear us apart. I simply wanted the happy marriage of which I dreamed. We were not the same people we were when we married. We were kids. We married at such an early age despite what people told us.

The "bubble" that I grew up in made life for me even more challenging. I feel as though I was so sheltered that I never saw the true essence of the hurt and pain of this world. I did not know how to deal with issues I never grew up around or had any affiliation with. Although my soul longed to be truly loved, admired, and happy, I told myself I had made my bed; therefore, I had to sleep in it. I felt stuck.

I cried so many days because I was in a place in my life where I was not happy at work or at home. Something had to give. I would drop my kids off at school and cry on the way to work because I did not know how I was going to continue in job I disliked for twenty-plus more years. I needed happiness somewhere in my life. I came home unhappy and left work unhappy. I never felt fulfilled. I never felt accomplished. I never felt needed. I cried out to God many times on my drive to work asking Him what my purpose in this life was. I sure did not know what my purpose on this earth was. I felt as though I was being punished for making bad decisions. I was reaping the consequences of insecurities and low self-esteem.

If you feel or have felt like this before, know that God is not mad, disappointed, or out to get you. God loves you! God does not hurt us. It is because of the sin of this world that we endure such pain and hardships.

I had been approached by a friend and asked to apply for an opening at her school, but it just did not feel right at the time. I looked into going back to school and getting a different degree. Everything I had any interest in, though, required clinicals, and I would not be able to pursue school without quitting my job. So that ended any hope of me getting a different degree, and I had no idea what I was going to do. Nothing felt right, but I could not continue in the job I was currently in.

As another year came and went, I was approached again by the same friend but asked to apply for a different opening at the school where she worked. As soon as she told me about the position, I knew I had to apply. It felt completely right, unlike the year before when she approached me. Little did I know that God was preparing my path. He was opening doors that would become my saving grace in the most challenging years of my life.

I rediscovered my love and my passion that next year. I was doing what I was meant to do, and that was to teach and be with elementary kids. I just had not found the right school and administration yet. I found it the moment I was offered the job. I had found happiness again. I felt as though I could do life now.

My marriage was hard many days, but I had found happiness in my job. Bringing happiness from work to home would make a difference. Or so I thought.

After months of asking my ex and pleading for what was going on—questioning what I was doing wrong or what I could do to make things better—the words I so dreaded but knew deep down at some point would come into existence were spoken. "I am done. I am tired of fighting for us anymore." Those words. That night. Waves were left that continue to keep crashing in. Just about when I am standing up from getting knocked down, another wave comes barreling in, sometimes holding my head under water and leaving me gasping to get a breath.

The emotional roller coaster began that night, and I have not yet been able to get off. I hope one day the emotional roller coaster will stop, but many consequences follow with the choices we make in life. I could have begged and pleaded that night. I could have begged and pleaded the days after. I could not, though, and I would not. I had at least come to the place in my life where I refused to beg someone to be with me anymore. I needed people in my life that would choose to want me, not someone who I had to beg to be a part of my existence. I asked many times in the days that followed if divorce was what he wanted. And I was ready to stay and fight if he changed his mind. It was after those few days and some very hurtful words that a part of me had a peace about divorce. You can have peace about something but still be distraught, confused, and depressed all at the same time. The peace came from knowing the differences we had did not have to be shared anymore. The brokenness came, knowing what divorce would entail.

I had made my bed. I was ready to spend the rest of my life trying to make the best of the choices I had made. But with his words came a freedom I had so longed for. If I was being completely honest, divorce had crossed my mind many times. We should have gone through with the divorce five years before when we separated and filed for divorce. I was always too scared to say the word or go through with a divorce. I could never find the courage to leave. I never had the faith I could do it alone.

I was now staring face to face with the word I dreaded. Divorce left me with a broken heart but a restored soul and a joy I've never had. I thank him for doing the one thing I knew needed to happen, but I never had the courage to do on my own. Maybe that is odd to hear in the same sentence, but you will see later what I mean. He had said the words I was too afraid to say. He had made the decision for us. I wept desperately for my kids and how it would affect them. I wept for my dreams as a child of being married with kids coming to an end. There was a peace that came over me, and I knew that this was the best thing for our family, yet it hurt so much. You always dream of getting married, but who dreams of getting divorced?

I mourned a marriage that failed. I was devastated at where my life had ended up. I cried because of the hurt I had endured and the words that had torn me down. I had become somebody I did not like. I never loved myself, and now I did not even like myself. For the first time, I realized that my past did not dictate who I was or who I wanted to become. I could stay in my past, and even the present, and crawl deeper and deeper into the hole I was in, or I could begin healing a heart and a body that had been hurting for so many years.

I could not just stay at home and wallow in my tears for the days to come, so I went straight to my boss the next morning uncontrollably crying and not knowing where or how I was going to do this. You know how I said earlier that God was making a path for me? Well he had. He had orchestrated my kids and me to be exactly at the right place at the right time. Our school has housing for coaches and the superintendent. By the grace of God and a wonderful superintendent, he gave his house up so the kids and I would have a place to live.

We waited two weeks to tell our kids. You want to talk about awkward. We lived in the same house for two weeks. We kept things as normal as possible. Just a few days before the kids and I were to move out, we told the kids the devastating news. It was another conversation that has been one of the hardest for me to have. Looking into their eyes when their dad told them what was happening and hearing them cry for hours after telling them was heart-wrenching to the soul. I felt horrible. We, their parents, the ones who were supposed to protect them, were causing such pain. That night our kids were forced to embrace a life they were never meant to have.

God intended for us to do life together as husband and wife. God intended for us to be a family. We were breaking what God had designed. We as a society give up. When things get tough, we quit. Not many choose to stay in for the long haul. We have allowed ourselves to be the most important thing instead of God. When someone does us wrong or does not see it our way, we quickly throw them to the curb in hopes that they get what they deserve. Once you choose to do life with someone else, it no longer is about you. The other person becomes your focus. And once you have kids, it has nothing to do with either one of you. So why do so many parents choose to use their children as leverage or punishment with their former spouse? It is heartbreaking to me. Divorce will have a lasting effect on the lives of our children, no matter their age. Whether it is love, trust, anxiety, security, depression, or stress, divorce is traumatic, and it affects the way we process things. It affects our future relationships. A child already has enough pain to deal with in divorce alone. So why add more hurt and pain to their precious souls? I have seen the hurt and pain divorce brings on the kids in my classroom as well as my own children.

From that very night, I chose to handle our divorce with grace. For my kids and even for myself, I needed God to be seen. It has not been easy, and I have failed many times, but I continue to strive to be God's light. I try my best to not let the words or actions I see allow me to say or do something in the moment because I am so upset that I will later regret. You must find a healthy way to release the frustration and the emotions that keep you from maintaining composure.

I understand this can be easier said than done. It takes a lot of willpower some days. Some days I do not have the willpower, and my words and actions are released with fury. What am I accomplishing, though, by saying these hateful words or losing my cool? Temporarily I may find relief. It may give me a satisfaction I have desired, but in the end, nothing is resolved. Nothing is better. I am left with the same emotions.

Grace can be hard to exhibit, but I was and am determined to show my kids how life can be with divorced parents. Some things come with divorce that we as parents cannot take away—the things a mother gives and provides that a father does not and vice versa. We had already hurt our kids enough. We did not want to add to more of their pain. My prayers then and even now are that God's light is shown through all of this. I want my kids to see love even when the world says I should seek vengeance.

Divorce is by far the hardest thing I have had to endure in my life. It has surpassed the death of a parent and rape. It has led from one incident to another. Every few months seems to bring on another obstacle. And each obstacle brings another wave of emotions. In my failures and mistakes, I can see my past for what it was and strive to make my future better. I am inflicted with trials because of the choices of my past, but I also have chosen to find the wisdom in what the past has to offer. My faith in God and my hope for tomorrow far exceed previous times. It has taken me being broken for the best of me to come to life.

Scriptures to Reflect On

So do not throw away your confidence; it will be richly rewarded. You need to persevere so that when you have done the will of God, you will receive what he has promised. (Hebrews 10:35–36)

Anyone who listens to the word and does not do what it says is like someone who looks at his face in the mirror and, after looking at himself, goes away and immediately forgets what he looks like. (James 1:23)

Chapter 5

Out of My Control

It's like the favorite sweater you wear in the winter—the one you want to buy in every color. It is so soft, warm, and comfortable. It is your weekend wardrobe for the season. One day while you are cleaning, you lean against the wall. You get caught on a nail. A nail that should have been taken out of the wall long ago, but you were going to get to it another day. You were just going about your day not knowing your favorite sweater was about to possibly meet its doom day.

As you pull away from the nail, the sweater begins to unravel. You at that very moment have the choice whether to stop and unhook yourself from the nail or to continue to pull the sweater as well as yourself away from the wall. If you choose to stop, you either call for assistance to get yourself unstuck, or you do it yourself. The sweater is easier to fix if you take the time to stop as soon as you realize something has a hold of you. You can pull the piece that is unraveling back in through the sweater, and you would never know it had been snagged. But if you choose to keep pulling away from the wall, your favorite sweater is no longer a sweater. It becomes a jumbled-up mess of yarn unraveling so much of the sweater that it cannot be repaired nearly as easily, if at all. The way you reacted when your sweater got stuck on the wall determined what was left of your sweater.

It is the same way in our lives. Some things in this world are beyond our control. We do not anticipate these things. They catch us off guard. They derail our plans, our thoughts, and our lives. A sweater being unraveled and ruined is no comparison to the immense seasons of our lives, which catch us off guard. We all have circumstances we did not anticipate. It can be from the evident things in life such as death, cancer, layoffs, and illness to even the smallest of things we try to take control of ourselves, but in reality, we have no control over anything.

I have found myself many times trying to fulfill my own desires instead of allowing God to decide. I get so frustrated waiting on His timing that I begin to take matters into my own hands. I know many times what the end result will be, yet I choose to not be still and listen. I might be left with an instant satisfaction, but in the long run, me trying to control whatever it may be will only set me further back from my destiny.

After my divorce I found myself longing for another person in my life. Many days I wanted and needed affection from someone. I wanted to be loved. Some men reached out to me, who I know could have satisfied my need for affection. It was hard. There were nights and days it was unbearably hard to not just give in. I had to daily—and sometimes multiple times a day—tell myself that it would only be a short-lived satisfaction. All it would do was set me back even further than I already was and add one more component to my anxiety and depression. "Everyone's toil is for their mouth, yet their appetite is never satisfied" (Ecclesiastes 6:7).

I found myself praying deliberately and repeatedly to God, pleading with Him to put things into motion and allow me to take minute by minute, hour by hour, day by day and to stop worrying about tomorrow and the days, months, and years to come. I pleaded, I yelled, and I cried to God. I desperately needed God to answer my cries to Him. When I look back now, I was talking to God like a three-year-old and throwing a fit because I was not getting my way. I am so thankful for the mercies and grace our Father shows us no matter our words or emotions.

There is always something throwing a hiccup in my day being a teacher. I plan and prepare for hours, and then a meeting comes up, or there is a last-minute assembly. A kid in my classroom throws up or has a bloody nose. A student asks a question that I did not anticipate, and I am engulfed in a conversation that takes up more time than I have planned.

I have learned to just roll with it. My schedule is always changing, and sometimes I do not get to everything I had planned for the day. I could allow myself to get all bent out of shape and let it ruin my day or even the plans I have for the rest of the day. Or I could just go with what life throws my way and stay focused on what my job is and what I am supposed to be doing.

It is the same way with your life. You cannot control certain things that happen to you or that are said to you, but you can control the way you react. If you are not careful, one thing after another can leave your life spiraling out of control. It is so easy for the devil to grasp us when we feel our lives unraveling right before our own eyes. You have the control to stay focused on God and to continue to strive for Him during all your brokenness and confusion. Friend, I know it is extremely hard to stay focused on God and to know He is good when one thing after another keeps occurring in your life.

As a teacher, I have seen many parents and their children. The apple typically does not fall far from the tree. Whether it is something positive or something negative, the kids resemble their parents. It is our jobs as mothers to show and exhibit an attitude of grace and compassion. We must show our children in a world of hurt that whenever things are out of our control, we do not have to lose it. We do not have to feel as though our lives are over and we have no future. God is good. When the world we live in is nowhere near good, God is forever good. Stop focusing on all the brokenness of the world and of your life; rather, focus on the good of God.

God answered my prayers. God let me have my way with the things I prayed and talked to Him about. He gave me everything I asked for. I got married just like I dreamed of as a little girl. I had a husband who had a great job. We had a nice home and nice things. I myself had a job. I had a precious son and daughter. Just like I had prayed to God for and wished for as a child. Yet I was unhappy. I was miserable. It was not as pretty and awesome as I thought it was going to be once I got it.

We complain so much over this and that, yet we are the very ones who add burden upon burden. We make it our job to fulfill whatever desire we have. We make it our will, not His. We end the day overwhelmed and exhausted. Our brokenness leaves us reaching for anything and everything that will make us happy. Yet all it does is add more brokenness. We look for happiness through our worldly desires. But those never give us the lasting fulfillment we so long for. So, we complain and blame God for it all.

We tend to think God is out to get us because of our past choices. We think we are being punished. We are not being punished, but there are consequences for our choices and for our actions and words. I forever thought my dad dying was because of what I allowed to take place with the man I trusted. I since have learned and know otherwise. The consequences we must face are not always immediate, and sometimes they not only affect us but the ones we love. We may not even be affected by the consequences, but the generations after us are affected.

We validate our habits—the things that we know we should stop doing. We validate the things we choose to do or use to cope with life. We can justify anything we want to make it right. We say because something happened to us as children or even as adults, we now can do or act certain ways. We do this to make ourselves feel better, and it justifies the reason for what we are doing.

I am guilty of validating the relationship I am in now to the relationships my kids' dad has been in. I think our relationships since our divorce have been completely different. I hold myself up to a different standard. There are some things we are both doing similarly, but I find ways to justify how they are different. I justify how I am right and how he is wrong. I am not any better.

Sometimes it takes our brokenness for us to relinquish all control and give it to God. It has taken my brokenness and complete exhaustion emotionally, mentally, and physically to say that I give control to God over every aspect of my life. God knows my needs. I think I know what I need, but many times I have been shown differently the things I believed I needed but really did not. God knows my heart and desires, and it is only through Him that I am changed and reborn. When I step all the way back and give God complete control, I pray my eyes see the vision God has for my life and my ears listen for the path I am to take.

Allow God to be the one in complete control. He will open doors where doors need to be opened, and He will close doors that need to be closed. Remember God sees the whole picture, whereas we see only in the moment. If a door closes, do not lose hope. Hang on to Him!

Is this easy to do? For me it was not. I saw people who said they gave it all to God—their problems and their emotions. They would say how free they felt. It was a weight being taken off their shoulders. They were able to breathe again without feeling suffocated.

I wanted so badly to be able to just give whatever it was over to God. It took me thirty-five years to finally get to the point where I could completely, without a doubt, look people in the eyes and say God has this even when I do not understand it one bit.

I have come to realize there are many things on this earth I am not meant to understand, but God will see me through it just as He has seen me through everything else in my life. There finally came a point where I could not try to be in control anymore. The more I tried to make things go my way, the more my life unraveled. The more I forced something, the more hurt came along.

My dad's death was out of my control. Although, it took me years to believe his death had nothing to do with my past decisions or the selfish girl who just had to drive the nicer, cooler vehicle. My dad had served his purpose here on this earth, and he was called home that Wednesday afternoon.

My dad baptized me when I was twelve—one of the most special moments I will treasure with my dad. My brother was nine years old and had gone to church camp for the first time the summer my dad passed away. He wanted to be baptized, and I remember thinking to myself that he was not ready—that he at the age of nine did not fully understand what he was doing. It was not my place nor is it anyone else's place to judge where someone else is in his or her heart. My dad baptized my brother in a horse trough at that camp session. A few weeks later my Dad was killed in a car accident. To this day, I firmly believe his purpose was to baptize and bring both his children to Christ. He had fulfilled his destiny here on earth and was then called home.

After my divorce was finalized, my uncle passed away from a brain tumor he was diagnosed with only a few months before. A couple of months after that, my mama, who seemed just fine, passed away in her sleep one night. Then a few months after my mama's passing, my cousin who was a year younger than me drank too much one night and passed away. This all took place in a nine-month span. That emotional roller coaster I was on only intensified in speed, turns, and drops. It left me realizing that no matter where I was and where I wanted my life to go, it was not going to happen the way I dreamed.

I thought that once I was divorced, life would become easier. As I said previously, there was a peace that came from the divorce. But just like all decisions, consequences follow the choices we make. Because I chose divorce, even with the positives that came from it, there has been heartache and tears. It is never ending and never will be. But with all that has transpired in the last few years, when the road turns before I see it, when there is a hurdle I must jump, and even when I find myself free falling off a cliff, I firmly believe and know God is in control. I tell myself every day that God sees the bigger picture. It is all in his timing, not mine.

We become stuck in the brokenness our past has created, the pain we are enduring right now, and the purposelessness of what is ahead if we are not careful. There are knots in our soul that we long to have undone. We must take the things breaking us and set them free. Do not be held down by the chains of hurt, disappointment, and fear. We will never fully maximize our purpose here on this earth when we allow these chains to keep us down. When we see no possible end to the circumstances we are in or the hurt we are enduring, give it to God. Give it to the One who knows all and sees all.

If you are in a season of need or feeling helpless, know God is here. He is walking right there along with you. A lot of times carrying you, but He is waiting on you! Waiting for you to call on His name and give it *all* to God. Not just give the parts you want to give and keep the parts you want to control, but to give Him every piece of your life. Your spiritual, mental, physical, and emotional parts of *you*!

God shows such mercy on us. He spares our hearts from knowing too much. If we knew what our future held—if we knew what was right around the next turn— we would not have the strength or the courage to move forward into the fire. He only shows us what we can handle in a certain time, all because of God's wisdom.

If I had known what my life would entail before the age of thirty-five, I would have told you there was no way I would make it through. I would not have the strength, the wisdom, or the endurance to get through it. I would not be yelling, "Bring it on!" I would be pleading for circumstances to not happen and choices to not be made. There is a very good chance I would have crawled in a hole and never came back out. For God's mercy, I am beyond thankful.

I have always been told that God would never give me more than I can handle. I do not believe in that statement at all. I believe God has allowed more to happen to me than I felt like I could handle. It was at that very moment when I was pushed further than I could handle that I learned to depend on God, on God alone, and no one else. I have learned to show up with willingness and do what I can do to keep going, knowing God will do the rest.

That means I take care of my responsibilities. I keep fighting. I continue to have a warrior spirit even when I lose vision because the pain sets in. I am no longer fighting alone but with God. Instead of trying to control situations and circumstances, control your focus on God. Get into His Word. Lean on Him. Talk to God throughout the day. When I give God control, He leads me to my destiny. Allow God to fight the battle He was always intended to fight.

I think about where life has taken me— where the roads have been extremely windy at times, where the mountains lead only to a straight cliff that falls into the crashing waves, and where the hole feels way too deep to ever climb out. I never imagined my life where it is today. I have endured hardships I have never wanted to endure and circumstances I never dreamed I would be a part of. I would not wish some of my hardships of life on my worst enemy. Although life has taken me down roads I never wanted to go—some by choice and others just because of the broken world we live in—I have come out with my head held high, a self-esteem I never had, and most importantly, a relationship with our heavenly Father that surpasses any relationship I will ever have on this earth. It was not easy. It was extremely hard at times. I have had many days where I was ready to throw in the towel and give up on life. But it was those gut-wrenching, take you down to your knees days and nights of crying, clinging to the smallest of things, giving everything you had to put one foot in front of the other days and experiences when I came to realize life is not how I ever imagined it to be. Most things I would never want to endure, but those very things have sculpted me and made me into who and what I am. It is our choice to decide if we allow the very things this world says should break us, tear us down, and make us feel unworthy and unwanted to break us. Or do we allow those very same things to build us and guide us into the person God has created us to be? Maybe it is the things in life that were meant to break us—or in fact have broken us—that are the very things setting us on the path to our divine calling here on this earth!

Scripture to Reflect On

So do not fear, for I am with you; do not be dismayed, for I am your God. I will strengthen you and help you; I will uphold you with my righteous hand. (Isaiah 41:10)

The Lord himself goes before you and will be with you; he will never leave you nor forsake you. Do not be afraid; do not be discouraged. (Deuteronomy 31:8)

In the same way, the Spirit helps us in our weakness. We do not know what we ought to pray for, but the Spirit himself intercedes for us through wordless groans. (Romans 8:26)

Consider it pure joy, my brothers and sisters, whenever you face trials of many kinds, because you know that the testing of your faith produces perseverance. (James 1:2–3)

I have told you these things, so that in me you may have peace. In this world you will have trouble. But take heart! I have overcome the world. (John 16:33)

Everyone's toil is for their mouth, yet their appetite is never satisfied. (Ecclesiastes 6:7)

Chapter 6

Loving Myself

As I look at my reflection in the mirror, I realize how much I have aged over the past few years. Where I went from being the smallest I have ever been to weighing the most I ever have. Now parts of my body touch that never have before. My age truly shows. I am embracing the parts of me I have struggled to even like, and for the first time, I can say I love me! I love the person I have become in the past thirty-five years. It did not happen overnight, and some days I must look in the mirror and tell myself why I love me. I respect myself now and know my worth in a world where we are left to feel unworthy because of our past.

We must discover where our hurt comes from and why we feel so broken before we can ever begin to heal and love ourselves. There are many reasons we find ourselves broken and unsatisfied with who we are or what we have become. You may be hurting because your marriage failed, an addiction took hold, you lost your job, the people who you thought were your friends left you, or whatever it may be. You must get more specific; dig deep into your soul. Pull out the boxes that have spiderwebs and dust covering them because you put them so far in the back of your head trying to forget the pain they caused—trying to forget the memories that left you feeling hopeless.

For me, what happened weeks before my dad's death twenty years ago has weighed heavy on my heart for all these years. My mind has been filled with guilt allowing me to not love myself.

As a society we put so much blame on the woman when she says she was raped. Society is good at pointing fingers and saying the girl or woman asked for it. Really? They ask to be violated? They asked for their innocence to be taken away? Rape is life altering. There is physical and emotional trauma left to endure the rest of their lives. No means *no*. Period. It does not matter what they were wearing, where they were at, or what they were drinking. When the word *no* comes out of a girl or woman's mouth, then all activity should stop. If it does not stop, then it is rape.

So many girls and women have been sexually assaulted or abused. Many more than we could fathom. Rape leaves you feeling dirty, unworthy, and used. For many it is embarrassing. They carry shame that rape has happened to them. They carry guilt like I did for so long because I allowed such an act to happen.

A daughter, a wife, and now a mother was molested as a child. To this day she struggles with the demons that haunt her from her molestation. Decades have gone by since she was molested, and she still cannot publicly talk about it. These are the words she has written and has wanted many times to express but cannot find the courage to say. "Over and over, salt has been poured into my gapping wounds. I tried over and over to explain to myself why a boy nine years older than me would think it was okay to put his hands in my pants on more than one occasion. I tried to find out what was wrong with me. How could something like that happen? I kept it to myself for ten years. Over twenty years later, I still cannot talk about it openly. I have no evidence it happened. I have no proof. No one to corroborate my story. Only my words and my memory. As a victim of sexual assault, when I hear people claiming the victim is a liar, I hear that I am a liar. When I hear there is no proof, so the offender is innocent, I think to myself, *I have no proof, so my abuser must be innocent too.* My voice stays silent because I am scared. I am embarrassed. I do not want it to hurt the people it would. I do not want the people to say, "Why now?" She depicts what so many girls and women feel.

I should have noticed when certain activities were over, I was always the last one to be dropped off, no matter how out of the way it was. Comments were made about how pretty I was. If he were in high school, he would date me. He was always asking me to come hang out with his family. Those are just a few of the red flags I should have noticed looking back.

It has taken me up until the last few years to not justify what happened and say the words, "I was raped." I was a child. He was an adult. I said no, and he continued. It played into my self-esteem and worth afterward.

I can now relate to so many hurting girls and women who have experienced similar situations. I was talking to a young girl just the other day, telling her about this book and my story, when she broke down in tears. She had been raped herself. The only ones who knew about it were her parents. She was carrying so many different emotions that no one knew about. Our paths cross numerous times a year, and it was not until I opened up and became vulnerable that we were able to better connect. You can be sitting in a roomful of people but feel completely alone. If we were to open our hearts and become more vulnerable, we would realize how many people sitting in the room are dealing or have dealt with some of the same things. And maybe, instead of turning down a self-destructive path, we could better navigate the demons that haunt so many of us and channel them into something positive.

If you are anything like me, it has been a challenge to love myself. Yes, there are some things I do love about myself, but there are many more things I do not love about myself. At times I have hid from others because my past has taken a toll on me and left me feeling worthless and ashamed. I get discouraged by what my body has become or what it never was or will be. How many times do we allow our mistakes to haunt us and keep us from loving the good, the bad, and even the ugly—physically and figuratively?

I struggle to love the less desirable parts of my body, and it can become a daily battle to not compare and desire someone else's body or traits. The thing that you want from somebody else may be the very thing that person wishes she did not have. Some would give anything to have a flatter stomach, long skinny legs, a bigger butt, a bigger chest, to be tall, or to be tanned. Then there are the very opposite who would give anything to have a smaller butt, a smaller chest, or to be shorter.

I am fairly tall, and I have always had skinny legs—or as I call them, "chicken legs." I am very self-conscious of them. I am also very pale. I always joke that you might need sunglasses when my legs are showing because you might be blinded. I have a hard time wearing shorts or dresses that show a lot of my legs because of this. Yet I constantly have friends who say they would love to have my legs.

I have naturally curly hair. It is one of those things that if you have it you hate it, and if you do not have it you want it. The underneath part of my hair curls differently from the top part of my hair. Then you add the fizziness, and, ugh, I do not like it. Yet the older I get, the more I am trying to embrace the natural beauty with which God has blessed me. But many days I do not feel like my wavy hair is such a blessing.

Our sense of beauty and self-confidence comes from within ourselves. A perfect body is not required to have fun. We all can carry ourselves with confidence. Size does not dictate our worth, beauty, or the amount of joy we deserve. The most beautiful woman is one who emanates confidence and radiates joy no matter her size.

We allow our weight, cellulite, stomachs, wrinkles, varicose veins, stretch marks, and many other things about our bodies to determine our happiness. We are so good at saying, "I will be happy when I lose ten pounds," or, "When I get my body more toned and my stomach flatter, I will be happy." We have got to begin loving ourselves even when we are not happy with where our bodies have ended up. We must choose to love the body that has gotten us to this point in life and be grateful!

The stretch marks and the baby bumps that never go away are left from bringing life into this world. Where mothers complain and wish the baby bumps would disappear, there is a woman wishing for the very thing we want to vanish. The rough and calloused hands and feet show a woman who has worked, who has gotten dirty, and who has become much stronger mentally and physically. The gray hair so many do not want to embrace, me especially, signifies you have gone through life. You have endured, and you have gained wisdom over the years. You are getting older. No matter how much we want to fight it, it is going to happen.

Loving yourself goes way deeper than the outward physical appearance. It's more than just my body weight, how short or tall I am, the color of my skin, my hair, and so on and so on. It goes much deeper. The inner beauty a woman has brings forth a radiating beauty both inwardly and outwardly. God made you to be unique in your own kind of way. There is far more to beauty than your physical appearance. Some of the most gorgeous women can become the most unattractive by their inward beauty. The way a woman treats others and speaks to them shows her true beauty. The way a woman handles an ugly situation with grace and composure as opposed to throwing out curse words and going crazy exhibits self-control and leaves a radiant essence about a woman. A woman who speaks truth instead of lies reveals a woman of integrity and respect.

I must learn to love and embrace the mannerisms and features that I was genetically given that I never asked for. As I get older, I say and do things my mom said and did with me. When we are all together as a big family, it is always joked around that I am my mom, who has become my grandmother. There is nothing wrong with that. But some things I would like to do or see differently than my mom or my grandmother. Because it is part of my genetics, it becomes very easy for my mannerisms and the things I say to be like them. It takes effort, usually a lot of effort, to see or change the things we want different.

It comes down to our human soul wanting to be loved. It is something we long for, especially if it is something you have never had. There are different kinds of love: a mother's love, a father's love, a child's love, family love, friendship love, church love, and spousal love. We look for love in many ways, and when we are not receiving the love we so desperately long for, we begin looking elsewhere. We typically end up loving ourselves less and less while we search aimlessly for the love we never had the opportunity to have or have lost.

So how in a world of social media that emits perfection, happiness, and the fairy tale life we so long for but cannot seem to get a hold of, do we begin to love ourselves outwardly and inwardly? How do we love ourselves and the things that have caused us so much hurt and pain? How do we find the joy we so long for when confronted by the very things we have every reason to be depressed about, to be resentful of, to be bitter about, to have anxiety over, and to fear, along with many more emotions that hit us at our core and can cause us to fall into a life of misery?

So many times I have found myself feeling as though I have failed in every aspect of my life. Many days I found myself screaming at the top of my lungs at my children and unleashing on them all my frustrations. I was able to keep my composure when out in public, but the first thing they did at home that I did not agree with or when they did not listen to me, I was screaming my head off. I look back at those years when my tone of voice came out of frustration and in essence only hurt and crushed the souls of my precious children.

I allowed my circumstances to dictate my attitude and determine if my day was good or bad. The eggshells I walked on many days and the moods I tried to not set off were soon the very things my kids were doing with me. I have guilt I carry for the way I acted as an exhausted, frazzled mother trying to keep my life looking as if I had it all together, even though every piece of my life was falling apart. Every role I was—mother, wife, daughter, sister, friend, and teacher—was nowhere near where I thought I would be in life. It was all so much harder than I ever imagined.

Happiness is not about finding the right person. A person is where I always thought my happiness would come from. It is what I had always yearned for. I had always put my happiness in someone else's hands. I allowed other people and circumstances to dictate my happiness. If another person is at the center of your focus, and that person is responsible for your happiness, you are always going to be miserable.

Happiness rather comes by striving to be the right person. You must be the right person in your heart. Only then are you able to have the right person in your life. The purpose of love or a relationship should not be based on someone completing you. It took me thirty-four years to realize I did not need someone to complete me.

It took me realizing that my life starts now, not when someone comes into my life. I can get in the pity party days of what I do not have and what I want, but my focus needs to be on the things I have right now at this moment. Focus on the blessings not the trials! God knows what I need. He will provide what I need at the time I need it, not any earlier or later.

We try to love people, but we aren't even whole within ourselves. If you do not believe that God loves and accepts you, then you will not be able to accept anyone else's view of you. You cannot even accept the way you are because you don't love yourself.

In a world where love is defined by others and materialistic things, I pray we begin to truly love ourselves and align our hearts with God's heart and His purpose for us! Even when we are not sure what our purpose is yet, remember that God made you just as He wanted you to be. You are loved for who you are, not what you do! This world needs you and everything you bring! God is good! God knows what we need! God has what we need!

To the desperate, broken woman who struggles to find happiness in the midst of an overwhelmed heart, I pray you find *joy*!

Happiness is an emotion that we feel. It is based on people, places, and things. You are happy when things are going well and when circumstances go the way you want.

Joy comes from within. It is about making peace with who you are, why you are, and how you are! No matter the circumstances and no matter the suffering, joy remains indefinite.

You may not be happy with where this journey of life has taken you—relationships that have failed, an addiction that has taken hold and you cannot seem to overcome, parenthood, a job you hate, rejection, loneliness, abandonment, or feeling lost. These are only a few paths life has taken so many of us on.

When a certain person, situation, or place may find you overwhelmed, stuck, anxious, depressed, angry, or bitter, look for even the smallest of things in which to find joy. You have the choice! The choice to dwell in the emotions, trials, and brokenness or the choice to let the same emotions, trials, and brokenness bring you joy through all the confusion and pain. It is about soul searching and finding the person you never knew you were or maybe even finding the person you once were but somehow lost. Whereas happiness falters, joy is constant! Choose *joy*! Consider it pure joy, my brothers and sister, whenever you face trials of many kinds, because you know the testing of your faith produces perseverance. (James 1:2-3)

With God you are fully loved. And because you are fully loved, there needs to be no fear of rejection. Nothing you can do will ever turn God from you. We may turn from God ourselves because we think we have done the worst thing ever, but our loving, gracious, sovereign God does not work like that. We orchestrate in our minds the things that are unforgivable. Society labels us because of our actions. There are choices we would have made differently. Yet there is a God who wipes our slates clean and who does not keep a running record of our faults. We must believe this and accept it from God. God loves you no matter what you did years ago or what you did yesterday. Because you are loved, you are welcomed home. You are worthy of love. You have a purpose.

When we strive for perfection, we will always find ourselves disappointed. Whether it is in a relationship, being a mother, your position at work, your appearance, or whatever it may be, perfection does not exist in this world. We must begin to love the things we dislike about our work, our relationships, our motherhood, and ourselves. Stop focusing on all the brokenness of the world and of your life, and focus on the good of God.

Girl, be who you are! Do not change because of someone's opinions of you. You do not need to sell yourself short and be someone else so that a certain group or person likes you. Do not be ashamed of your story. Your story is what helps you attain your purpose. Your story is what has gotten you to where you are today. Your story is what can save yourself and others. Embrace every part of your story, and love all of it. Even if your story is nowhere near what you ever wanted, know that it is exactly what you needed to be the woman you are today. Choose to take care of yourself and love yourself. You are no good to anyone else until you genuinely love yourself and accept who you are and what you have done, whether small or big.

Freedom occurs when you truly love yourself. I lost myself or maybe I never even knew myself because I was so hungry for love. I grabbed hold of anything or anyone who would show me that love. That meant not allowing myself any self-worth. I now see and understand how precious love is. It is so much more than a word or an action. God has a love for me that I could not grasp until I was able to hand everything—the good and the bad—completely to Him. He still loves me no matter how far off course I've gone or how many times I continue to mess up while trying do what is right.

So when I am in the dressing room crying and discouraged because nothing fits like it should, when I refuse to wear shorts because my legs are too skinny and too white, or when I choose to eat the Snickers bar and drink the Dr. Pepper instead of having the water, humus, and snapped peas, I choose to embrace it all. I choose to not let my insecurities keep the experiences and me from the memories to be made with family and friends. No more allowing my insecurities to define who I am when I have so many more important and positive names that I have worked so hard for: mom, wife, daughter, teacher, maid, referee, boss, coach, friend, author, and whatever other names fit.

It is about you embracing your imperfections and the less desirable parts of yourself! Do not allow others to define who you are, what you are capable of, where you are going, or when it will happen. Allow God to determine these things. Allow God to determine your worth. And let me just tell you, *you are worth it!*

Scriptures to Reflect On

You are altogether beautiful, my darling; there is no flaw in you. (Song of Songs 4:7)

For you created my inmost being; you knit me together in my mother's womb. I praise you because I am fearfully and wonderfully made; your works are wonderful, I know that full well. (Psalm 139:13–15)

But the Lord said to Samuel, "Do not consider his appearance or his height, for I have rejected him. The Lord does not look at the things people look at. People look at the outward appearance, but the Lord looks at the heart." (1 Samuel 16:7)

Chapter 7

Changing Me

C hange is inevitable, and whether you like it or not, change is going to happen. Change can be predetermined. You can choose to go on a diet to better your psyche and your health. You can choose to get married. You choose your job. You choose the words you speak. You can choose to stop smoking. You can choose to stop drinking. These all require a conscious effort, and you ultimately control the change taking place.

It is also natural for us to change. I am not the same person I was when I graduated high school. Thank goodness for that. And I will not be the same person I am today in ten years. We evolve and change over time.

Events in your life occur causing a change that was not intentional. When someone you love becomes ill and you are with them through their journey of sickness, it changes you. You learn to appreciate moments you used to take for granted. You realize just how precious life is. When you become a single parent, you have a different respect for those raising children alone. Death of a family member or a friend causes change. Life happens, and we are forced to change. More than likely that change happens when we least expect it, when our world is already crumbling apart, or our life already feels so overwhelmed. When everything around us is changing, remember God is still the same.

From my experiences, change typically ends up being a good thing. A lot of times I doubt, and I cannot wrap my mind around how change could even be a good thing. I have seen and felt firsthand the havoc change can cause in your life and how it can hinder you from your purpose if you are not willing to go through the process.

At times in my marriage I felt as if I was a single parent. After being a single parent for a few years now, there is a difference between doing everything alone married and doing everything alone divorced and single. Having another adult in the household made things easier. I could at least leave the house to take a breather when married. You cannot leave the house for a breather when you are by yourself with kids. I have had to change how I cope when the kids become overwhelming. When I need a break, I cannot just get in the car and go to Sonic and get a drink. I have learned to just step outside and walk to keep my agitation at ease.

Change can impact you negatively when you decide to take on the quest of changing someone else yourself, and that is exactly what I did. "Lord please turn his heart to you. Allow him to see the things that will make our marriage and our family flourish. Open his heart to the things You desire for him and for our relationship. Please, Lord, change his heart and thoughts. Change his desires. Mold him into the man you intend him to be and the man I desire him to be. Lord, please just open his eyes to my heart and allow him to see my hurt and my needs."

How many times have you prayed something similar trying to change someone else to meet the requirements or desires you feel they need to meet? How many prayers have you so desperately prayed pleading for God to change someone else's heart or thoughts?

I spent many hours praying that prayer daily. I prayed for years and years for God to change my husband and to break his heart so he would see what he had and where I longed for our marriage, our relationship, and our friendship to be. I became so discouraged, as I felt my prayer was never being answered. We would go months, and there were even a few good years. No matter how good it got, we always ended up back in the same rut.

There are multiple people in my life who I have tried to mold into what I wanted them to be. I have tried for years to change them.

I built the image of what and where they should be in my mind. I thought it was attainable for them.

If you are anything like me, you set out on this quest to change them. You put so much effort into trying to get them to see your way or to just be the person you want them to be that you forget about yourself. We put our focus on the wrong thing when we try to alter someone else to perfection instead of focusing on our own calling and God's pursuit of us.

If we go into any relationship thinking we can change someone, we are setting ourselves up for heartache and letdowns. A person changing comes only from his or her inner desire. It takes the work of that person to change. Changing someone else should never be your intention.

There comes a time in your life where you must live for *your* joy! Not the joy and happiness of others, but where *you*, no matter the decisions you make and the insecurities you may feel, find joy through it all. Change occurs because we allow it. We allow a transformation to begin taking place. Family, friends, and even strangers off the street are going to offer their advice. They are going to contribute their wisdom on you. I have found no matter how hard I try to verbally convey to others my emotions, my struggles, and even my desires, people do not understand my circumstances unless they have walked in my shoes. Even then, when our emotions, circumstances, struggles, and dreams align, they are still never exactly the same. I finally realized it was me who needed to be brought to my knees and changed. Kneeling on the floor was the exact thing I needed for change. Kneeling on my knees and pouring out my heart to God is what saved me.

During the wee hours of the morning once I was balled up on the floor pouring my heart out to God, pleading for understanding, when it occurred to me that it was definitely me who needed to change. My heart was broken and shattered. I cried out to God, "I just do not have it in me! I cannot do this anymore." I needed to be humbled and broken down to where there was nothing left to give in order to be refined into something new. That was exactly where I was. I did not have the energy to care anymore about what I wanted or even needed. I needed God to take full control of my life. I no longer had the desire to line my life out.

I needed my past and who I had become because of my past, but I also needed my soul to be renewed and given a fresh new start in life. I decided to put in the work for what I sought in this life. I grabbed a hold of what God had placed on my heart years ago and allowed God to start the process of my transformation.

My prayers changed, and I began fervently asking God to allow me to change—allowing me to undergo the soul surgery I needed in order to be the person God had destined me to be. I was so tired of living up to the expectations of what people said and thought.

Lord, change me. Help me to see the disappointments that once left me in heartache and resentment and allow me to release the negativity and the desire for revenge and just let it go. Lord, change me. Give me strength to forgive when my heart has been broken. Lord, change me. Allow my heart to love again as if it had never been broken. Allow me to trust again and only expect the best. Lord, change me to be your light even when the days are dark. Lord, change me to believe in you—to have an unwavering faith where I know your plans are for my best interest, and your timing is just when needed. Lord, change me to be content with the things I will never understand. Lord, hold me tight and change me!

I finally realized I did not have to stay stuck in my past or the things I have acquired from my past. We have the choice to change the things that have us feeling trapped and stuck. When we feel stuck, we become stagnant. When we become stagnant, we don't grow. You cannot better yourself if you never grow.

I had tried many times to change but never could. I wanted so desperately to try and make situations and myself better, but my trying got in the way of me trusting God. Trusting God when everything was not what I pictured.

Trust Him when your finances have left you drowning in debt. Trust Him when your marriage is on the rocks, and you are hanging on by a thread. Trust Him when your child is addicted to drugs. Trust Him when you are laid off. Trust Him when people reject you.

With our freedom of choice comes the choice to try and fix things or change situations on our own or to trust God and allow Him to change and mold us into what we were created to be.

I needed and wanted to remove the roadblocks that were keeping me from finding the essence of my purpose. I became so desperate for change but was terrified to change. I pleaded for God to show me the parts of me I did not know existed. Asking this of God would entail more heartache and more confusion in my life, but I discovered new dimensions of myself that I did not know were there. It took me out of my comfort zone.

Change may be hard—really hard. There will be opposition from the devil when you finally decide to change and allow God to truly take control. Change may cause you to become uncomfortable. It will stretch you more than you feel you can go. It will get you completely out of your comfort zone. Change takes place when your heart, your thoughts, and, most importantly, your actions make you uncomfortable. Your failures become lessons you learn from, and your mistakes allow you to grow.

I was the first one on my mom's side of the family to get a divorce. I cringed at what my family would think. I was the first of all my friends to get a divorce. I cringed at what my friends would think. What would the church think? I was living for everyone else's approval and not my joy. I was staying in a relationship where I felt defeated most days. Where our worlds were not the same. Who we had become since high school was very different from whom we are today.

A person does not know who he or she is or what life is even about when in high school or even college. We evolve into who we are as life experiences open doors and close others. As life tugs at our heartstrings we begin to really seek our passions and live for what we believe. For my marriage, those things went in different directions from one another.

With change comes the fear of rejection and the fear of what others will think. All my life I have been a people pleaser. I want everybody happy and want them to like me. I struggle when I know someone is upset with me or I sense a void between someone else and me. If I am not careful, I allow it to consume me and eat me alive. It keeps me up at night, and it takes my mind captive during the day. I wonder the what-ifs and the could-haves.

For some, in order to change, you must get out of the shadow cast upon you. Some of us place ourselves in that shadow. Sometimes others place us in the shadow. It might be a family member who just seems to have it all together—is successful and always excels in everything he or she does. Maybe it is the very opposite, and you feel as if you are being identified because of a family member's bad decisions. Maybe it is a job position where you have taken over from someone who was exceptional, and now you feel as though you have huge shoes to fill. Maybe it is a past relationship where you are afraid of the same scenarios occurring. I think it is human nature to compare ourselves to others. When we are living in the shadow of someone else, we believe we are the same. The truth is that none of us are the same. Therefore, we do not need to compare ourselves to the victories or failures of others. You will stay miserable and feel unworthy until you stop living in the shadow of someone else.

I was raised in the shadow of church—one way to worship and one church of which to be a part. It was all I ever knew growing up. Once I became an adult, I continued with what I knew. I continued with what I was comfortable with. After attending other denominational churches, I realized parts of me were not being fed. I felt more connected to God in a different worship experience. It has been hard for me to go to another denominational church when my entire family is a different denomination.

I had to stop living in the shadow of where others thought I should go. I know there has been disappointment in my choices. It was more important for me to have my heart and soul fed and encouraged than to stay in the mold I felt I was supposed to fit into. Disappointment from others is more than likely going to follow when you choose to live for yourself and not where or how others think you should live or be. When you are living for God and your relationship is with Him, many will not understand.

I have built relationships in both denominations. They both inspire me and keep me going. It has taken me digging down deep for courage, but I have overcome the shadow that for many years kept me imprisoned to others' thoughts and expectations.

When you choose to embrace change you are also choosing to become vulnerable. People may not understand what you are doing or why you are doing it. In all honesty, it is not anyone else's business but yours. You choose who you allow to see your heart and your struggles. Sometimes change involves growing thick skin and finding out who your true friends are and what kind of family you have.

When I chose to let my son go live with his dad, people looked at me and questioned me as if I was crazy. Then when the straw broke the camel's back, and I had my son come back to live with me, I had a whole other group of people who questioned me and made me feel rejected.

My son needs that male bonding time and craves boy things that I cannot provide. It breaks my heart that my son would rather live with his dad. It breaks my heart that he has to choose who he wants to be with, too. That is a choice he should not have to make. So, I allow change to happen, and it hurts straight down to the core, but it is not about my happiness but the joy and success of my son.

Anytime you are seeking change—no matter if it is your job, your thoughts, your words, your behavior, or whatever else it may be—you are seeking something better. You want the best for yourself, your family, or someone else. As we change, others may not see it as good or may not like who you are becoming. We risk losing people we thought were our friends and sometimes even family. There will be storms and relationships lost, but remember that change will require you to get rid of old habits, old thinking, and old behavior.

I began embracing the choices of my past that had led me to my knees crying out to God. I was no longer talking myself out of better just because of what my story told. I wanted to be God's light—where people saw Him through me. Do not let this world, the job, the people you come into contact with daily, or even your relationships define who you are. Be your own kind of special! You only fit within the box your mind creates. Throw away the box. Do not set a limit of where you can be and what you can become. The sky is the limit, and God can far exceed any change your heart desires. Allow God to use your failures, your disappointment, your brokenness, your love, and your joy to change *you*!

I had created in my mind this wonderful life that was becoming harder and harder to attain. As I set forth on the path to change, my days became harder before they got better. Self-doubt would hold me down many days. I questioned what was wrong with me. Crying became my second nature. I held tight to God, my friends, my family, and my colleagues. My views of myself and what I viewed of others began to change. I embraced a life I never wanted.

I found joy amid the hardships. I chose grace instead of revenge. Instead of fighting the emotions and the circumstances coming my way, I took each one as it came. I laughed instead of crying. I found the positive when everything seemed negative. I spoke positivity.

I do not have it together, nor will I ever, but the holes of my heart that I have longed to be filled are now being filled with the knowledge of God. We are in constant communication throughout the day, and I am in his word. I have scriptures all over my bathroom so that when I am getting ready in the morning, I read them and reflect on them. I have scripture and prayer on my computer at work and on my visor in my car. Put his word wherever you are. When it gets tough. When anxiety starts to come to the surface. When you debate if change is even possible. When you question if you have what it takes to change. Step back. Pray. Read scripture. Be still. Listen. Be patient. Pray.

Friend you can do it! You've got this! God's got you!

Scriptures to Reflect On

The righteous cry out, and the Lord hears them; he delivers them from all their troubles. The Lord is close to the brokenhearted and saves those who are crushed in spirit. (Psalm 34:17–18)

Therefore, if anyone is in Christ, the new creation has come: The old has gone, the new is here! (2 Corinthians 5:17)

I was pushed back and about to fall, but the Lord helped me. The Lord is my strength and my defense; he has become my salvation. (Psalm 118:13–14)

So then, just as you received Christ Jesus as Lord, continue to live your lives in him, rooted and built up in him, strengthened in the faith as you were taught, and overflowing with thankfulness. (Colossians 2: 6–7)

Chapter 8

Friends

We have been that obnoxious group of girls in the restaurant who have the booming laughter that carries throughout the entire building and leaves the whole restaurant staring at us. We have laughed so hard until we cried and almost wet our pants. Maybe some of us have wet our pants. We have spent days and nights crying with one another because of hurt and pain in our lives. We have had sleepovers with our kids because life was unraveling faster than we could grasp at times. We have stuck with each other through thick and thin. When cities and states separate us. When we do not see eye to eye. Our friendships have remained intact and have only grown stronger as the years have gone by.

This is not what my friendships looked like growing up. Growing up, I did not really have many friends. The lack of friends came from me being so shy. The lack of friends also stemmed from a social awkwardness. I never knew how to interact or speak with others. It was not something that came natural to me. It is still something I struggle with today. You have your go-to questions, but carrying on a conversation with someone I do not know or hardly know is extremely difficult for me. Therefore, the awkwardness remained and still does to this day.

I have always heard and was always told it was the friends I would make in college that would become my lifelong friends. I do keep in touch with a few of my college friends, but people I went to high school with have become my tribe. People who were once just acquaintances have become the best of friends. They have become my rock. They mean the world to me, and I could not have gotten though these last few years without them.

How often do we let the rumors we have heard about someone shape our minds into who we perceive someone to be before we even meet him or her? How the person you could not stand would be the person who you could not do life without.

It is so easy to put the walls up like I have talked about in previous chapters or to judge the person by the way he or she talks, dresses, or interacts with you. God, though, has an interesting way of bringing people into our lives whom we did not know we needed.

I think of one friend who from the first minute I met her I did not care for her. It was the way she responded when I spoke to her. It turned me away, and I chose to judge her based on a few minutes of interaction. We would occasionally run into each other and simply share the irrelevant small talk of "How are you doing?" I was just being polite. How many times do we do this with people? We carry on a fake conversation because we "have" to. We talk to them because it would be rude if we did not. Sometimes we miss out on the amazing qualities of an individual because our minds are shut off to his or her unfamiliarity.

When I started a new job, the first person I saw when I walked into the building was her—the girl who I could not stand. I rolled my eyes, and I thought to myself, *Oh, great! I have to work with her!*

Since we worked together, I was forced to communicate with her. It was an eye-opening experience for me because she was nothing that I made her out to be. We quickly became inseparable. Our husbands both worked evening shifts, so we were together from the time we left work until our husbands got off from work. We confided in one another and experienced life together.

This unanticipated friendship has now been in place for thirteen years. We have spent eleven of those years living hundreds of miles away from each other. No matter the distance or time apart, we come together and pick up just as if we had seen each other the day before.

A friend is always there. A friend will surprise you with lunch on Valentine's Day because she knows you are alone. A friend calls your doctor to ask the nurse to follow up with you because she is concerned about your emotional state. Friends are the ones who show up at your house when you are done with life and left in a fog. They force you into the car to go get a Sonic drink. They drive around with you knowing that at that very moment you are mad at them for dragging you out of the house. As a friend, you allow that person to be mad knowing that one day he or she will thank you for it.

Friends ease your stress. They know the right words to say and the right food and drink to bring when comfort is what you need. Friends bring us joy that no one else can. Friendships bring a social connection between one another that prevents us from loneliness and isolation.

There is no way I could have gotten through these past few years without my friends. They have been my rock many days. They have encouraged me on days when I felt like a failure. They have loved me unconditionally. They have improved my mood. When I am down, nervous, or angry, they have a positive way to boost my mood and improve my outlook. They have supported me through tough times, even if it is just to vent or share my problems with them.

There is nothing better than having a group of friends you can shoot out a text to asking for prayers, and you know they are on their knees in an instant. I can always count on my tribe to immediately send requests to God. Having friends with a faith like yours only brings you closer to God and each other. Friends who can hold hands and talk to God together are a bond to cherish.

Friendships are work, just like any relationship. It takes effort on both parts. It takes putting differences aside, and sometimes even hurt, to see friends flourish. Friendship is respecting one another even when we think the other person's choices are not the best. We may give our opinion, but no matter the decision made, we respect the one making the decision. We have each other's backs no matter what. We take each other under our wings and know we will never fall alone.

Our tribe has been taking a girls' trip each year for over ten years. It is a valuable time that we all look forward to, but with the fun trips and girls' nights come heartache and turmoil. Our thirties have kicked our butts. They have pushed us. Challenged us. Tested us beyond our knowledge.

The past few years we have experienced severe depression, loss of parents, loss of a child, divorce, addiction, diagnoses of lifelong illnesses, and hormone imbalances. Through these past few years our bond has grown deeper. It is not just with one person or even two. It is a group of women whose lives have intertwined with one another. It is something very rare and special. Something we do not take for granted. We find ourselves talking about how blessed we truly are to have the friendship we do.

I also have those friendships that come and go, just as you do too. Someone comes into our lives for just a short period of time and then leaves. That brief friendship may lead to a connection later in life. The friendship that leaves you wondering why this person was in your life for such a short period of time may have just been your saving grace during a certain season of life. There is no doubt in my mind that God crosses our paths and intertwines our stories for something far greater than our eyes can see.

My divorce was finalized at the end of the school year. That summer was beyond tough. That is when miles of walking became my norm. When I sat inside at home, I felt like the walls were closing in on me. As a new school year started, I was weary and lonely. We were starting a new program, and our district brought in a woman who would mentor us. God provided a godly woman in my life who impacted me more than just in the classroom but in my personal life. Her sweet messages and notes she would send me were the very things I needed to get through that school year.

She had experienced some of the things I was going through. Where her story had a different ending than mine will have, she related to me. She understood my pain and my frustrations. She was a shoulder to lean on during the hardest year of my life. She wrote 1 Peter 5:10 and placed it in a picture frame. The verse: "And the God of all grace, who called you to his eternal glory in Christ, after you have suffered a little while, will himself restore you and make you strong, firm, and steadfast," sits in my kitchen, and I read it multiple times a day. It is a reminder that my suffering has its reasoning, and I have become so much stronger and wiser from it. This too shall pass, and good will come from my pain.

I can think back to college and previous jobs I have worked. Those people who were there became my friends, even if just for a short time, and all have taught me something. Some inspired me and encouraged me to be better. Others allowed me to see who or what I did not want to be. They also allowed me to see others' stories and where they have come from. I have been enlightened into worlds I had never known.

I had to put myself out there with other people to be inspired but to also be hurt. Nobody wants to be hurt, especially by a friend. We must build these relationships even when hesitancy takes over because of the fear of being hurt. Isolation brings pessimism; relationships bring hope. I know I have said this many times throughout this book, but we are not meant to do life alone. For many years I was alone. I became so fixed on judging every person whom I befriended. I needed them to meet my needs. I had this picture in my head of how my friendships should be. I chose what they saw and knew about me. I did not want to invest in any friendship because I did not want to be hurt or judged.

It took a confrontation between one of my best friends and I before I realized my friendship with one friend was not the same as another girlfriend. We all have different needs. It is the same as a marriage. I can go days, sometimes even weeks, without talking to friends. Life just seems to keep me busy. I have good intentions, but when I think about shooting a friend a text or calling her it is late at night. Then I have friends who talk daily with one another. When you look at both friendships, it should not be surprising that the ones who converse daily are always doing something together. They always know what is going on in each other's life.

For me, though, it was hard, and I pulled away for a few months. It was then I realized our needs in a friendship were different, and it is okay. You must invest where you want to gain. If I wanted to be in the know, then I had to put forth the effort to reach more often. I am okay now when friends go and do, and I am not a part of it, because at the end of the day my needs are being met.

I feel this chapter is me teasing you with a Cookie Monster from Cheddars. I am sitting right in front of you eating the yumminess of the warm chocolate chip cookie with the melting ice cream, chocolate syrup, and nuts with no care in the world. I do not offer you one single bite, not even the cherry. I am not bragging about my friendships. It is something that did not happen overnight. A few started in school, but so many more have been acquired as the years go by, and life happens. (By the way, if you have not tried a Cookie Monster, go get one as soon as possible. Yummy!)

My prayer, my friend, is that you can break down barriers and allow a girlfriend into your soul. You will put forth the effort and build a trust where you can be completely vulnerable. I pray I am giving you hope that there are people out there with whom you can connect. If you have not found them yet, do not give up. Keep looking. They are out there. If you have even one friend who is your go-to person and who understands you, cherish that friendship and continue to put the work into that relationship so your friendship only grows stronger.

Once I allowed my friends to see and know every part of me, and once my friends became vulnerable as well, our bonds quickly changed. We are a safe place where we can let our guard down and our hearts can open. By the grace of God, we have made beauty from the ashes in our lives through our friendships, and I could not be more grateful.

"Close circles of friends are important. When we avoid these things, we drift into isolation and leave ourselves open to battles we should never have to fight alone. We should surround ourselves with a circle of people to do life with. A circle that stays with us through the easy times and the hard times."—Dave Winn

Scriptures to Reflect On

A friend loves at all times, and a brother is born for a time of adversity. (Proverbs 17:17)

One who has unreliable friends soon comes to ruin, but there is a friend who sticks closer than a brother. (Proverbs 18:24)

Do not make friends with a hot tempered person, do not associate with easily angered, or you may learn their ways and get yourself ensnared. (Proverbs 22:24–25)

Two are better than one, because they have a good return for their labor. If either of them falls down, one can help the other up. But pity anyone who falls and has no one to help them up. (Ecclesiastes 4:9–10)

Chapter 9

More Emotions

I needed one place I could go and be alone—one place where I could cry. I could not hold back the tears any longer. I went to the bathroom where I wished and hoped no one would follow me. The water works began—uncontrollable sobs. Seconds later I heard footsteps coming my way. Trying to not let my kids know when I was upset and crying, I stuck my head in the laundry hamper. Actually, it was more like half my body was in the laundry hamper. "Mom, what are you doing?" asked my daughter. I choked back tears and cleared my throat.

"I am looking for a shirt," I said.

"Oh, okay", she said as she left the bathroom. My sobs continued with my head hanging in the laundry hamper of clothes. If putting my head in a hamper of dirty, stinky clothes was how I hid my emotions, then that was how I cried.

I needed to cry. I tried so many days to hold my emotions in until I got the kids in bed, but there were days it was not easy at all. My head has been in the laundry hamper more than I would like to admit. I wanted my kids to see me strong. I did not want my kids looking back at these years and remembering their mom crying all the time. I believe children need to see their parents' emotions. My children have seen me cry some but not hysterically and not with negativity about their father. It has been important to me since day one that I do not talk negatively to my children about their father no matter what is going on or my own thoughts about him.

The first year after my divorce was hard. I was flooded with so many emotions. I have always been emotional, but I have never experienced the emotions that came with divorce. So many emotions at one time needed navigating. Even though there was a peace that came with my divorce, it still left many questions and emotions that took a toll on me mentally and physically.

Living in a small town, everyone knows you and your business. And if they do not know your business, they will soon. It got to where I would not go to the store during the day. I would wait until the late hours of the night to go because of fear of running into someone. Most people meant well, I knew they did, but asking me the why, what, and when questions left me with so much anxiety. I would pull into the grocery store parking lot to sit there for minutes trying to talk myself into going into the store only to drive away and go back home.

For the first time in my life I learned what anxiety attacks were all about. I learned how they could just happen for no apparent reason. My chest felt like it was caving in, and my heart was about to beat out of my chest. I never realized what people meant when I heard them say how their anxiety would leave them debilitated. Now I understand it. I have felt and seen firsthand just how debilitating anxiety can be. It is not something you just get over or can snap out of. It consumes every breath you take as you feel all the walls closing in on you.

I went on a girls' trip one weekend up to the mountains. We laughed and had the best time ever. It was a much needed, relaxing time away. As we got a couple of hours from home, my heart started pounding. My anxiety triggered, and I was back to reality.

It was nice to get away, but we cannot run from our circumstances. We can take a break—we can get away—but at some point, you must face reality again. I had to learn how to navigate with and through the anxiety I felt during the day and even during the night at times. There have been many times I questioned if I was nearing the end because everything was closing in, and I could not catch my breath. That is a very scary and helpless feeling when everything seems to be closing in on you and there is nothing you can do.

I have already mentioned how I struggled with depression in high school. I could not let myself get back to that low of a place again. I had two children who depended on me. I tried for a couple of months once our divorce was over to handle my emotions and everything on my own. I wanted to seem to others as indestructible. Even though reality had me shattered. I wanted to be able to do things and handle things on my own. I could do it! So I thought.

The fact was I could not do it. I needed help! It hit me when I took my son to the doctor. While talking to the doctor about my son's diagnoses, I started crying. Ugly crying. Hyperventilating crying. It was at that point the doctor had my kids go sit with his receptionist. As my doctor handed me tissues, I poured my weary emotions out to him. He did not rush me out. He did not get upset because I was now messing up all his appointments for the rest of the day. He took time to hear the desperation of a mother trying to keep it all together. He listened. He cared. In that office that day I realized how broken I was. Others' perceptions of me could not matter anymore. I had to take care of myself.

I have never been a pill taker. To this day I still gag when I must swallow huge pills. I was a senior in high school putting vitamins under my tongue after breakfast and pretending to swallow them. I would then go spit them in the toilet and flush them because I could not swallow those huge things. The struggle was real. I could not even swallow a small ibuprofen until I was in college. This was one reason I fought for so long to not have to take any kind of medicine. Silly, I know.

I have never judged anyone who has taken medicine for their emotions, but I was determined I would not be a person who needed medicine. I gaged thinking of having to take pills daily, and I knew I could handle life on my own. The depression I struggled with since high school was mild, and I was able to get myself out of it within a few months. I was going to be able to do the same thing this time as I did any other time depression knocked on the door. This time was way different; my emotions were too extreme.

I had to face the fact that for me to be my best for my own children, I had to get on medicine. Depression is serious and just as debilitating as anxiety and other mental health disorders. I am a firm believer now in medicine when it is taken correctly and used for the right reasons. I needed help balancing my emotions.

Medicine is not a cure-all, but I needed help coping with the emotional roller coaster I was experiencing. I was not only an emotional basket case; I could not sleep either. Once I did fall asleep, I would have nightmares or wake up in full-blown anxiety attacks. I found it very ironic that the girl who was so desperate to not be alone and craving love ended up exactly where she was fifteen years ago, alone and searching for love. The only difference is that now I see and know what true love is. Love is much more than a feeling.

I also had to find a way to release my emotions and my anxiety. I had already started walking some, usually a mile or two. But as reality of a single mom set in, walking became my only escape. As homework and one kid or the other crying every night and kids themselves not sleeping, walking became my sanity. There were weeks I would walk forty miles. Many walks I cried. Many walks I poured my heart out to God. It did not matter the weather or the time of day. I would walk in the heat of the summer or the brisk cold air of winter. I would walk in the light of the day or the dark of the night. It was how I coped for the first year or so.

I encourage you to find a healthy way to release anger, anxiety, or whatever emotion feels as if it is eating you alive. Whether it is walking, running, reading, coloring, meditating, or kickboxing, just do something to release your emotions. I have held my emotions in a few times, and then comes the one thing, the straw that broke the camel's back, and I am hurling out all my emotions at once. It is not pretty. I am sure many of you have experienced the same outcome when keeping your emotions bottled up. Many words are said that hurt others. Words are spoken in an ugly way when they could have been spoken in a more healthy and constructive way.

I found myself many days discouraged. I had a preacher that once said, "Be careful what you pray for. I prayed for patience, so God gave me twins." So, I have never asked for patience. LOL. Your impatience can be your greatest enemy, but it can also be your greatest strength. God was teaching me patience even though I never asked for it. God knew it was what I needed. He has been teaching it to me for the last couple of years. Where I once wanted to fulfill my own happiness, God has shown me how to stop eagerly wishing for something and just slow down and watch the amazing things he has in store unfold.

My experiences and emotions have allowed me to come to a whole different outlook and respect for single parents. As a teacher, I have a better understanding for the single parent who struggles to get all kids' homework done and who at the end of the day just cannot do it. Many nights the first year my son and I would both be crying out of frustration because of homework. You have no one to tag and say, "It's your turn." Or the night my daughter was sleepwalking and broke her hand at one in the morning. We spent hours in the ER and still all went to school the same day because I had meetings I could not afford to miss at work. People are so quick to judge and speculate. Sometimes single parents are truly doing the very best they can. When you think a parent does not care? They do. They just literally have nothing left to give at that moment.

I am not making excuses for single parents. There is a difference in a parent who is trying to be the best parent he or she can be and still fall short and the parent who makes excuses and holds no accountability to his or her child or the child's actions. If you are a single parent trying the best you can to manage your emotions as well as your children's, keep pushing forward. One day your children will see the love you have spent pouring into them. Single parenting is not for the faint of heart. That is a fact!

We all deal with different emotions. We experience emotions that leave us full of energy and ready to tackle the day. Then we have emotions that leave us drained and barely functioning. Our emotions determine our mood and how we interact with people. Our emotions dictate our day—whether it is a good day or a bad day. I have days where I allow one small hiccup to ruin my entire day, and my mood is foul to everyone with whom I come into contact. When something does not go as planned, I choose to allow anger and frustration to ruin my day, but then I have had days where I have every reason to let my day be ruined, yet I choose to keep a smile on my face. I embrace the situation or what has changed and stay in a positive mood. It is my choice whether to let the unpleasant circumstances steal my joy.

I have always been a planner. I used to get so worked up and aggravated when things did not align like I had planned. I would get mad when people did not react the way I felt they should. I have experienced enough in life that I now am grateful if anything I have planned goes even remotely as planned. I now expect things to change and my expectations and plans to not be met. And that is okay. I just have to laugh now when things do not go as I expect, and just take it as it is and go with it. Otherwise I would cry. And I have done enough of that to last many lifetimes.

Emotions also dictate how our time is spent and how we spend our money. When I am dealing with the emotions of fear, anxiety, or depression, I find myself isolated and withdrawn. That is a pretty accurate description for someone dealing with those emotions. But living weeks, months, and even years of isolation leaves you feeling abandoned when everyone else continues moving forward in life. Then when someone or something wakes you up, and you decide to live again, it can feel extremely overwhelming to catch up and make up the time you let get away from you.

When I am down, I find myself buying unnecessary things for myself. It makes me feel good to have new things, especially clothes. Many nights I have found myself online ordering clothes for my kids or myself because it is an instant feel good. When I should be saving my money, I am spending it.

Just as it takes time and effort to change our circumstances or situations to have true meaningful friendships, it takes time and effort to not allow an emotion to control us. It is okay to feel any emotion, but it is not healthy or productive to stay in a negative emotion for a long period of time.

Ask for help from doctors, friends, family, a counselor, or a preacher. I promise you are not alone in any emotion you are feeling.

You would be surprised the number of people who are feeling the same way you are at this moment.

Lean on God; stay true to his word. The best way to calm your emotion is to have scripture to go to. Place scripture and positive quotes all around so when you feel the negativity of your emotions sucking you in, you may reflect on the powerful positive words. Remember that instant change will more than likely not take place, but the more you are in God's word, the more vulnerable you become, the more positivity you surround yourself with, the better your emotions become.

If you are around someone who is negative all the time, chances are at some point you will become negative as well. If you are around someone who is positive and joyful, it becomes much harder to be stuck in your negativity all the time. I lived in a house where patience was very slim. Yelling occurred many times a day. I found myself becoming the parent I did not want to be. I was becoming what I was a part of. Deep down it was not who I wanted to be, but it was so hard to not allow my unhappiness to dictate my mood. I did not want to be yelled at, but I was yelling at my kids because I did not want them to do something wrong. I had very little patience myself. Things as simple as spilled milk on the table or floor would send me over the edge and screaming my head off at my children as if I myself had never spilled milk.

Throughout this book I have talked about emotions I have felt, and I am sure you have felt many of these same emotions. Emotions are powerful. Some we need help with. Some we need assistance navigating. Do not let yourself stay focused on the negative emotions. You are not defeated. You are just on a setback ready for a comeback. Smile instead of frowning. Laugh instead of crying. Remember you choose your own *joy*!

Scriptures to Reflect On

He gives strength to the weary and increases the power of the weak. (Isaiah 40:29)

"For I know the plans I have for you," declares the Lord, "plans to prosper you and not to harm you, plans to give you hope and a future." (Jeremiah 29:11)

Come to me, all who are weary and burdened, and I will give you rest. (Matthew 11:28)

I will refresh the weary and satisfy the faint. (Jeremiah 31:25)

The Lord is close to the brokenhearted and saves those who are crushed in spirit. (Psalm 34:18)

I sought the Lord, and he answered me; he delivered me from all my fears. Those who look to him are radiant; their faces are never covered from shame. (Psalm 34:4–5)

For we do not have a high priest who is unable to empathize with our weaknesses, but we have one who has been tempted in every way, just as we are—yet he did not sin. (Hebrews 4:15)

When anxiety was great within me, your consolation brought me joy. (Psalm 94:19)

I can do all this through him who gives me strength. (Philippians 4:13)

Chapter 10

Being on Hold

I absolutely dread anytime I must call a business or organization and know it will be forever before I talk to a human being. You call and go through all the automated programming. The last thing they ever tell you is the number to push to talk to an actual person. And if I try to push 0 too soon they will say it is an invalid response. Then you have others where you speak into the phone and apparently when you have a Texan accent, they cannot understand you. I end up being directed to a department I do not need to talk to. Sometimes you wait on hold for hours being diverted from one department to another. If you are having a really bad day, your call is dropped after being on hold for hours to only get to start the process all over again. I would rather stick my head in a door and close it—not really, but you get what I mean. I am sure you have wanted to do the same thing.

It is so frustrating when you are on hold. How hard can it be for someone to pick up on the other end of the line and answer your question or fix your problem? You put in so much time waiting on hold when you could have been doing something else. Whether it is doing something else for fun or doing something productive, time seems especially wasted when your problem is not fixed, or your question is left unanswered. You spend all that time on the phone for what?

This is the same with us in life. Seasons and situations of life seem to be put on hold. During these times of our lives we become so frustrated with waiting. It is so hard to put forth the effort when it feels and looks as though nothing is happening. I struggle at times to see that God is still with me. On the days I doubt, I yearn for God to show me he sees my heart and has a plan for me. When I am so desperate to see the light at the end of the tunnel, I ask God for my spirit to be awakened.

I need God to nudge me in the direction I need to go. But after making so many wrong decisions and being hurt time after time, doubt takes hold of my mind. I am sure, friend, that this is something you have struggled with yourself, often feeling as though you are taking three steps forward only to take four steps back.

You still get out of bed even though your mind and body long for rest. Your soul is weary and hurting, yet you choose to put your feet on the ground and face yet another day. You keep living even when you question why. You do not understand. Yet you decide to keep fighting even though the blows of life keep knocking you down.

I tucked my son into bed one night just as I always do, and he asked a question that left me pondering life myself. "Mom, you know how Dave has preached about us being on hold? Well, I think I am on hold. I think we are on hold."

"And why do you think that?" I asked.

"Well God is not answering my prayers. I have asked God to help me with my grades and my work at school. It is just not getting any better. It is still hard, and I still have troubles. Then Daddy's and your divorce; I never thought I would have to go through this. Everyone in our family is dying, and my friend is hurting. When will it be better?"

I tried so hard to have the right "church" answer. But that night I did not have the answer to tell my son. In my heart and mind, I was asking the same question. I cried myself to sleep nightly asking the question my own child was pondering.

After the divorce, family members passing, and a friend my son's age being diagnosed with cancer, I would tell my son that we were in a season. A season of hurt that soon would pass. Would it, though? I got to where when I told him that, I could not believe the very thing I was telling him. God was fixing everyone else, while our lives just kept falling apart.

Many days I found it hard to stay obedient to God. I questioned why God was working in everyone else's lives and not mine. I had cried and pleaded for God to let our season of hurt be over. Yet it continued to be one thing after another. It was not fair. Did God not see how bad my kids and I were hurting?

I felt as though I was getting nowhere in life, and my ex was out living carefree while I was left to deal with life, with my emotions, and also with the kids' emotions. There is nothing worse than watching your own children hurt and suffer, especially when you are the cause of it. My kids were having to endure a part of life they were never meant to endure.

I debated many days on turning my back and walking away from God. But the days I would start to turn, there was a tugging at my heart, a voice in my head pleading for me to keep hanging on. Keep hanging on even if it was by one thread because eventually that one thread would be woven back into a rope that would save my life.

Sometimes the reason we struggle to receive the destiny God has set out before us is because we do not have our priorities aligned. Life was all about me. I was selfish and longed for my happiness most days. For years I talked to God when I needed Him. When everything was okay or even with the little struggles that came my way, I would figure it out on my own. My relationship with God was on a need-to-know basis. I talked to Him when I needed Him. Otherwise I did not talk to Him.

If we are not careful we only reach out to God when things are bad or good and we do not have a daily relationship with Him. We are not putting Him at the forefront of our lives. We feel so often that we have been placed on the back burner and forgotten when a lot of times it us who place God on the back burner. We call on Him when our lives are slipping through our fingers and expect Him to come to our rescue. What we interpret as God not listening or God not answering is a lack of prioritization in our lives.

I am guilty of this. Many times I have prayed when things got bad. I would summon God into my life, and when he did not come sweeping in like my knight in shining armor, I would become upset and angry with Him. I only talked to God when I had a problem or when I wanted something to change.

When we align our hearts with God's heart and our plans with his purpose, he will give us things! It may not be exactly what you are wanting or even come close to what you were thinking, but he will provide. Your focus is where it starts. What you magnify, you get more of. When you lean fully on God, he makes a way.

You cannot focus on the past. What is done is done. It cannot be changed. Accept it and move on. You cannot focus on the future. Yes, you can set goals, and you can have dreams to strive for, but you must get through today before you can get to your future. We must focus on the now! Tomorrow is a wonderful place to be. Tomorrow can take my worry and anxiety away and temporarily be my get away from life. It comes down though to your focus, and the only way to tomorrow is through today. I've got to live *today*—not the what ifs, the could haves, or the might bes.

I continued praying. I continued being in God's word. I continued to have hope. I chose to accept that maybe this season was not just about hurt and brokenness but about God preparing me. I chose to accept that maybe this season was going to be longer than I wanted, and God had his reason for it.

What was God preparing me for?

At the time I had no idea, but I knew God had never left me, and he never would. When I felt like he was not there, it was those days that he was carrying me. My emotions and vulnerability were soaring as my faith became indestructible. I was taking blows left and right, yet I knew in full confidence that God had me. He was allowing—and still is to this very day—things to happen that knock me down. I may take a few days to be knocked down, but I rise back up and tell Satan to back off. He may bring me down temporarily, but he has nothing on me. Satan will collapse! God will prevail!

I do not have a green thumb at all. My kids no longer get me plants because I cannot keep any plant alive to save my own life. Anytime someone suggests me getting a plant, my kids are quick to let any and everyone know that it will die. I either forget to water, or I overwater the plants. I have come to love fake succulents and greenery. It looks nice, and I do not have to try and keep something else alive. Many days I am thankful to have fed two kids and two dogs.

In the front of my house I have yellow irises. Because I cannot keep a plant alive, I know nothing about flowers. I just thought it was some grass plant when I first moved into my house. Then in the spring these stalks began to grow, which then produced this beautiful yellow flower. I was very sad when I realized the flower only lived for two to three weeks.

Now year after year, each spring, these beautiful yellow irises bloom. And for about three weeks I get to enjoy their beauty. The rest of the year the irises go through their process so that they can grow and produce a beautiful flower when it is time for it to bloom. The process these flowers go through is invisible, yet the purpose for when they are to bloom always occurs.

This is the same for you. You have a purpose. It is still working even when you do not see it. Your uncertainty may leave you confused and unsure, but know you are still growing. Some things just take time. While you are waiting, instead of pitying yourself, work on yourself. Become the best you. Do not settle with who you are and what you have. Strive for more. Instead of feeling defeated and overwhelmed, treasure the time you have alone to find and see your strength, your worth, and your soul. Reflect on who you are, and where you have come from.

Relish in who and what you are becoming. In your most lonely and quiet seasons come your biggest victories. There is healing in your loneliness. Do not get discouraged when everyone around you is receiving what they prayed for. Do not become weary when you feel unheard and forgotten. You are loved, so while you feel as though you have been placed on the back burner, take this time to better you, so that when your time comes you are truly 110 percent *you*!

Remember God's grace. It is that grace that accounts for the years that you have wasted and the time that you lost. Grace accounts for the opportunities you have been given but did not know how to accomplish.

While God is growing and watering the seed that has been planted in you, allow yourself the rest you need, so when your harvest is ready, you are ready. You can give every part of you to being whomever he calls you to be and whatever he calls you to do. Allow God to unfold the purpose that he has for your life.

Scriptures to Reflect On

———————

Let perseverance finish its work so that you may be mature and complete, not lacking anything. If any of you lacks wisdom, you should ask God, who gives generously to all without finding fault, and it will be given to you. But when you ask, you must believe and not doubt, because the one who doubts is like a wave of the sea, blown and tossed by the wind. That person should not expect to receive anything from the Lord. Such a person is double minded and unstable in all they do. (James 1:4–8)

Never will I leave you; never will I forsake you. (Hebrews 13:5)

Yet I am always with you; you hold me by my right hand. You guide me with your counsel, and afterward you will take me into glory. (Psalm 73:23–24)

Now faith is confidence in what we hope for and assurance about what we do not see. (Hebrews 11: 1)

Do not let your hearts be troubled. You believe in God; believe also in me. (John 14:1)

Chapter 11

Glad It Happened

One morning as I drove my country route, I looked at the beauty and the calm around our town after the massive winds we experienced the day before. As I drove, I saw many roofs damaged, siding on houses falling off, trampolines mangled, and lawn décor ruined; things that once had a place had been uprooted and moved. Blue, sunny skies had become a brown fog of dust the night before, and it made me reflect on the last few years of my life.

If I had known what I would endure over the next few years, I would have told you I was done with life. I would have had no reason to get out of bed, to push forward, or to even try when I knew the heartache that was on the horizon. I am blessed I did not know what my future held.

We are blessed that we do not know what awaits us around the corner. If we were to know these things, many of us would not be able to put one foot in front of the other. We might choose not to live. God is saving us from more stress, confusion, and heartache than we are already enduring.

I dreamed of everything my life would entail and become. But after years of trying to meet my expectations and my dreams, I no longer had the energy or the desire to try anymore. I gave every part of my life and dreams to God. There are things I ask God for, but I completely trust Him—whether it goes the way I want, or it looks nothing like what I asked for.

I have gone from a full-fledged planner where when things did not go my way I would pout, get mad, and let it ruin the day and the experience. Now it is good if I even somewhat make it to what was planned or if it somewhat resembles what I had in mind. I am taking life as it comes and trying my best to handle things with grace. I do not always succeed, but my goal has been to show God's grace in the midst of turmoil and heartache. When the world says I have every right to be depressed, to throw in the towel, to be angry, to seek revenge, I am trying to enjoy the things that count and mean something. I am spending less time and effort dwelling on the things I cannot change. My time is not being wasted on things that in the grand scheme of life really do not matter.

I have been uprooted these past few years and moved to a different place. It is a place I've wanted to get to and I see others at, but I never imagined these were the things I would have to endure and experience to get there. I have had days where it took everything I had to get out of bed, where I have cried so much I didn't know how there could possibly be anymore tears left, where my emotions were a rollercoaster, where depression and anxiety took hold of me, and where I pleaded with God to fix it or take it away. As I still struggle with heartache and not understanding certain circumstances, I have learned that I am not meant to understand everything, but I must embrace it and trust that God knows exactly what he is doing! We must embrace our circumstances and our choices for each of us to fulfill what God has called us to be! We must be completely turned back to dust in order to be rebuilt into something so much greater! Most of the time God far exceeds the expectations and the ways we want or plan for ourselves! It just took more time and looked different than we ever imagined!

As I see a woman who went through a recent divorce and her ex-husband died shortly after their divorce, I ask why. She asks why. People ask why. From personal experience, divorce is the hardest thing I have had to endure. Divorce left so many more emotions and heartbreak than the death of someone. So why did God allow the hurt and the pain from the divorce to occur, to only take his life a little over a year from divorcing one other?

I do not understand it, but I firmly believe it allowed a woman who was dependent on others to become independent. She has learned to do things for herself that she had not done in decades. She found strength she did not know she had. She has established relationships since her divorce that will help her through the grieve of death.

Had her divorce not happened, she would be learning to navigate this new life while mourning the loss of someone with whom she has spent thirty-plus years of her life. While she still grieves the loss of a man that she spent over half her life with, she is better equipped to be there for her children, who are mourning the loss of their father. She already has people in place who can help navigate her through the days and years to come.

Our lives are not random. You are not placed here on this earth just by chance. There is a purpose—a reason for your existence. There is a reason for the joy and for the hurt that we endure. It is through the joy and pain that we can manifest God's plan. Know that you are stronger than you ever thought imaginable. On the days when you don't think you will make it, you will. I promise. It may be ugly, and you may feel all alone, but you will make it—one minute, one hour, one day, one week, one month, and one year at a time. The storm in your life may not end on your timing, but rest assured that God has amazing things in store for you. Your storm may seem never-ending, or your storm may continue building, but know there is good amidst all the hurt and pain, and God will use it toward your purpose in life.

I have watched people in my life who have struggled with addiction. These people have almost lost their families because of addiction. Their addiction, though, was their saving grace. Had they not gone through their addiction they would not be where they are in life today! They are serving God and are a testament to the power of God. Through their vulnerability, people are able to see how God always has a way to steer us back on course and find our purpose!

Allow yourself to be transformed by your vulnerability. We think people will judge us because of things we have done. And, yes, some people will judge and will speak negativity into your life. But do not let them be the ones who keep you silent. There are many more hurting people in this world who long for someone to relate to their feelings and their circumstances. Allow your pain and scars to help others.

Do not allow the feelings of bitterness and hatred to consume your life because you were dealt cards you never should have been dealt. Forgive those who have hurt you—who have caused you pain or led you down the path of destruction. Most importantly, forgive yourself. You will never be able to completely move on and begin new when you cannot forgive. I am not saying forgive and forget. The scars that are left will never go away. But when we allow ourselves to forgive, we no longer hold ourselves captive. We become free. We can move from hurt and bitterness into a newness of life.

God has placed precious gifts inside each of us. We must discover those gifts and use them to their full potential. God weaves our messes into something amazing when we trust the process for our purpose! Our life experiences are not just for our benefit and transformation but also for the benefit and transformation of others as well.

I always come back to the story in the Bible of Samson and Delilah. Samson was to be this amazing man who defeated the Philistines, but Samson falls in love with a Philistine woman—the enemy. Looking back, everything that took place with Samson had to happen in order to lead him to the next thing to come—in order for Samson to fulfill his purpose. It did not look the way Samson's parents envisioned it to be. They did not understand how their son was to defeat the Philistines when he married the enemy.

This is the same with us. We do not understand it most times, and many times our hearts are broken. Things are happening in a distinct way so that our purpose may be attained. Maybe what you are going through is the anchor for someone else's purpose. God intertwines our stories into a beautiful bouquet when we fully allow our stories to strengthen us instead of hindering us.

If life has you downhearted right now or your season of sorrow is yet to come, remember that God can give us anything. And he will, unless it is not best for us. He knows far more than any of us. The things in your life you never dreamed of or would not wish on your worst enemy are the exact things you needed to assist you to your purpose. Reach out and help other women so that they do not feel alone in the craziness of life. Do not be embarrassed and ashamed. Speak truth.

I live where I work. I drive a bus route for extra income. I am a single parent. Never did I think I would say those three sentences, but I am forever grateful for them. I have crossed paths with some amazing people who have left an imprint on my life. I will be forever grateful for these beautiful souls. This life of mine is nothing I ever wanted but is everything I needed.

As I write this book, I am faced with challenges daily where I must choose to continue to move forward and seek more for my life. One of my biggest fears has become reality—one of my children has decided to live with their dad. My heart has been shattered, and some days I must fight away the negative questions and thoughts I feed my mind.

I have no idea what my future holds for myself or for my children. I do not understand the whys, but I have faith God knows exactly what he is doing. Maybe this has nothing to do with my purpose but the purpose for my children. Maybe it is the exact thing my children need. Maybe it is the opportunities needed to discover the desires God has placed on my children's hearts.

As my story continues to be written, I give my life and my children's lives to God. He holds us in his hands. Jesus died a cruel death. He was brutally beaten, spat upon, and ridiculed. Yet it was a part of the plan. A part of a plan that gives us grace and frees us from our sins. Had Jesus not endured his hardship, we would not be saved. His pain is what fulfilled his purpose.

It is our pain and suffering that brings us to our purpose!

Scriptures to Reflect On

Do not conform to the pattern of this world, but be transformed by the renewing of your mind. Then you will be able to test and approve what God's will is—his good, pleasing and perfect will. (Romans 12:2)

Blessed is the one who perseveres under trial because, having stood the test, that person will receive the crown of life that the Lord has promised to those who love him. (James 1:12)

As a prisoner for the Lord, then, I urge you to live a life worthy of the calling you have received. (Ephesians 4:1)

From him the whole body, joined and held together by every supporting ligament, grows and builds itself up in love, as each part does its work. (Ephesians 4:16)

For we are God's handiwork, created in Christ Jesus to do good works, which God prepared in advance for us to do. (Ephesians 2:10)

For if you forgive other people when they sin against you, your heavenly Father will also forgive you. But if you do not forgive others their sins, your Father will not forgive your sins. (Matthew 6:14–15)

But we have this treasure in jars of clay to show that this all-surpassing power is from God and not from us. We are hard pressed on every side, but not crushed; perplexed, but not in despair; persecuted, but not abandoned; struck down, but not destroyed. (2 Corinthians 4:7–9)

Each of you should use whatever gift you have received to serve others, as faithful stewards of God's grace in its various forms. (1 Peter 4:10)

Acknowledgments

There have been many days when the devil has tried to convince me this book was not meant to be. I questioned if I was crazy for even attempting to write a book. How would I ever come up with enough words to write?

These family and friends have not only encouraged me but believed in me. Thank you from the bottom of my heart. I love you all!

Carson and Cambree, you are my pride and joy! I am blessed to be your mother and so proud of everything you have accomplished thus far in life.

Mom, I am beyond blessed to be your daughter. Thank you for guiding me and setting me on the right path to follow God.

Josh and Adrienne, thank you for your love and support in all I do! You two are a true example of loving like Christ.

Stephen, I could not have asked for a better man to come into my life and step in as a dad. Thank you for all you do for my kids and myself.

Corlie, Molly Beth, Kari Jo, Amanda, Whitney, Holli, Sara, and Randilyn, thank you for being my tribe. I could not do life without you girls!

Eric, thank you for coming into my kids and my life. You are the answer to so many prayers. It is so great to know gems are still out there.

Dave, thank you for your words of wisdom and the wonderful sermons you preach that always reach me right where I am at.

Halie, thank you for understanding me and always having an ear to listen.

Molly Beth Photography, thank you for seeing my vision through your amazing talent.

Elly, thank you for your encouragement through parenthood as well as life. Thank you for your friendship.

Molly, thank you for always being there no matter what. Thank you for the ongoing support you provide.

Dr. Haught, thank you for always encouraging and caring for my kids and me. You will always have a special place in my heart.

Heath, thank you for being an inspiration to me!

Lynn, Tonya, Lori and Dally, thank you for the support you have given me and the encouraging words you send my way.

Brittany S. and Brittani G., I am so thankful we can always pick up like it was just yesterday.

G-mom, G-dad, Craig, Deena, Lynzee, BA, Allyson, John, Donice, Amanda, Casey, Stephanie, Rod, Nancy, Yovonna, and Sydni, thank you for always loving me!

M.O.R.E. family, thank you for your encouragement and the wisdom you give. I always look forward to Tuesday nights!

Robyn, I am so thankful God placed you in my path. You not only helped me professionally but personally. You were a godsend!

Church family, thank you for your support and guidance through the storms of my life.

Dr. Schaffner, thank you for taking care of my children and me. Thank you for genuinely caring.

Scriptures

The New International Version has been used to quote scripture throughout the book. Here is a convenient guide to the scriptures cited in the book.

Chapter 1: The Past

Forget the former things; do not dwell on the past. See, I am doing a new thing! Now it springs up; do you not perceive it? I am making a way in the wilderness and streams in the wasteland. (Isaiah 43:18–19)

Let us hold unswervingly to the hope we profess, for he who promised is faithful. (Hebrews 10:23)

Brothers and sisters, I do not consider myself yet to have taken hold of it. But one thing I do: Forgetting what is behind and straining toward what is ahead, I press on toward the goal to win the prize for which God has called me heavenward in Christ Jesus. (Philippians 3: 13–14)

He heals the brokenhearted and binds up their wounds. (Psalm 147: 3)

Even though I walk through the darkest valley, I will fear no evil, for you are with me; your rod and your staff, they comfort me. (Psalm 23:4)

May the God of hope fill you with all joy and peace as you trust in him, so that you may overflow with hope by the power of the Holy Spirit. (Romans 15:13)

Chapter 2: Words

You hypocrite, first take the plank out of your own eye, and then you will see clearly to remove the speck from your brother's eye. (Mathew 7:5)

My dear brothers and sisters, take note of this: Everyone should be quick to listen, slow to speak and slow to become angry, because human anger does not produce the righteousness that God desires. (James 1:19–20)

Let your conversation be always full of grace, seasoned with salt, so that you may know how to answer everyone. (Colossians 4:6)

Do not let any wholesome talk come out of your mouths, but only what is helpful for building others up according to their needs, that it may benefit those who listen. (Ephesians 4:29)

Sin is not ended by multiplying words, but the prudent hold their tongues. (Proverbs 10:19)

The soothing tongue is a tree of life, but a perverse tongue crushes the spirit. (Proverbs 15:4)

The heart of the righteous weighs its answers, but the mouth of the wicked gushes evil. (Proverbs 15:28)

What goes into someone's mouth does not defile them, but what comes out of their mouth, that is what defiles them. (Matthew 15:11)

Those who guard their mouths and tongues keep themselves from calamity. (Proverbs 21:23)

Set a guard over my mouth, Lord; keep watch over the door of my lips. (Psalm 141:3)

The words of the reckless pierce like swords, but the tongue of the wise brings healing. (Proverbs 12:18)

A gentle answer turns away wrath, but a harsh word stirs up anger. The tongue of the wise adorns knowledge, but the mouth of the fool gushes folly. (Proverbs 15:1–2)

Chapter 3: Worldly Satisfaction

My flesh and my heart may fail, but God is the strength of my heart and my portion forever. (Psalm 73:26)

When tempted, no one should say, "God is tempting me." For God cannot be tempted by evil, nor does he tempt anyone; but each person is tempted when they are dragged away by their own evil desire and enticed. Then, after desire has conceived, it gives birth to sin; and sin, when it is full-grown, gives birth to death. (James 1:13–15)

For the grace of God has appeared that offers salvation to all people. It teaches us to say "No" to ungodliness and worldly passions, and to live self controlled, upright and godly lives in this present age. (Titus 2:11–12)

Do not conform to the pattern of this world, but be transformed by the renewing of your mind. Then you will be able to test and approve what God's will is –his good, pleasing and perfect will. (Romans 12:2)

Chapter 4: Made My Bed

So do not throw away your confidence; it will be richly rewarded. You need to persevere so that when you have done the will of God, you will receive what he has promised. (Hebrews 10:35–36)

Anyone who listens to the word and does not do what it says is like someone who looks at his face in the mirror and, after looking at himself, goes away and immediately forgets what he looks like. (James 1:23)

Chapter 5: Out of My Control

So do not fear, for I am with you; do not be dismayed, for I am your God. I will strengthen you and help you; I will uphold you with my righteous hand. (Isaiah 41:10)

The Lord himself goes before you and will be with you; he will never leave you nor forsake you. Do not be afraid; do not be discouraged. (Deuteronomy 31:8)

In the same way, the Spirit helps us in our weakness. We do not know what we ought to pray for, but the

Spirit himself intercedes for us through wordless groans. (Romans 8:26)

Consider it pure joy, my brothers and sisters, whenever you face trials of many kinds, because you know that the testing of your faith produces perseverance. (James 1:2–3)

I have told you these things, so that in me you may have peace. In this world you will have trouble. But take heart! I have overcome the world. (John 16:33)

Chapter 6: Loving Myself

You are altogether beautiful, my darling; there is no flaw in you. (Song of Songs 4:7)

For you created my inmost being; you knit me together in my mother's womb. I praise you because I am fearfully and wonderfully made; your works are wonderful, I know that full well. (Psalm 139:13–15)

But the Lord said to Samuel, "Do not consider his appearance or his height, for I have rejected him. The Lord does not look at the things people look at. People look at the outward appearance, but the Lord looks at the heart. (1 Samuel 16:7)

Chapter 7: Changing Me

The righteous cry out, and the Lord hears them; he delivers them from all their troubles. The Lord is close to the brokenhearted and saves those who are crushed in spirit. (Psalm 34:17–18)

Therefore, if anyone is in Christ, the new creation has come: The old has gone, the new is here! (2 Corinthians 5:17)

I was pushed back and about to fall, but the Lord helped me. The Lord is my strength and my defense; he has become my salvation. (Psalm 118:13–14)

So then, just as you received Christ Jesus as Lord, continue to live your lives in him, rooted and built up in him, strengthened in the faith as you were taught, and overflowing with thankfulness. (Colossians 2: 6–7)

Chapter 8: Friends

A friend loves at all times, and a brother is born for a time of adversity. (Proverbs 17:17)

One who has unreliable friends soon comes to ruin, but there is a friend who sticks closer than a brother. (Proverbs 18:24)

Do not make friends with a hot tempered person, do not associate with easily angered, or you may learn their ways and get yourself ensnared. (Proverbs 22:24–25)

Two are better that one, because they have a good return for their labor. If either of them falls down, one can help the other up. But pity anyone who falls and has no one to help them up. (Ecclesiastes 4:9–10)

Chapter 9: More Emotions

He gives strength to the weary and increases the power of the weak. (Isaiah 40:29)

"For I know the plans I have for you," declares the Lord, "plans to prosper you and not to harm you, plans to give you hope and a future." (Jeremiah 29:11)

Come to me, all who are weary and burdened, and I will give you rest. (Matthew 11:28)

I will refresh the weary and satisfy the faint. (Jeremiah 31:25)

The Lord is close to the brokenhearted and saves those who are crushed in spirit. (Psalm 34:18)

I sought the Lord, and he answered me; he delivered me from all my fears. Those who look to him are radiant; their faces are never covered from shame. (Psalm 34:4–5)

For we do not have a high priest who is unable to empathize with our weaknesses, but we have one who has been tempted in every way, just as we are—yet he did not sin. (Hebrews 4:15)

When anxiety was great within me, your consolation brought me joy. (Psalm 94:19)

I can do all this through him who gives me strength. (Philippians 4:13)

Chapter 10: Being on Hold

Let perseverance finish its work so that you may be mature and complete, not lacking anything. If any of you lacks wisdom, you should ask God, who gives generously to all without finding fault, and it will be given to you. But when you ask, you must believe and not doubt, because the one who doubts is like a wave of the sea, blown and tossed by the wind. That person should not expect to receive anything from the Lord. Such a person is double minded and unstable in all they do. (James 1:4–8)

Never will I leave you; never will I forsake you. (Hebrews 13:5)

Yet I am always with you; you hold me by my right hand. You guide me with your counsel, and afterward you will take me into glory. Psalm (73:23–24)

Now faith is confidence in what we hope for and assurance about what we do not see. (Hebrews 11:1)

Do not let your hearts be troubled. You believe in God; believe also in me. (John 14:1)

Chapter 11: Glad It Happened

Do not conform to the pattern of this world, but be transformed by the renewing of your mind. Then you will be able to test and approve what God's will is – his good, pleasing and perfect will. (Romans 12:2)

Blessed is the one who perseveres under trial because, having stood the test, that person will receive the crown of life that the Lord has promised to those who love him. (James 1:12)

As a prisoner for the Lord, then, I urge you to live a life worthy of the calling you have received. (Ephesians 4:1)

From him the whole body, joined and held together by every supporting ligament, grows and builds itself up in love, as each part does its work. (Ephesians 4:16)

For we are God's handiwork, created in Christ Jesus to do good works, which God prepared in advance for us to do. (Ephesians 2:10)

For if you forgive other people when they sin against you, your heavenly Father will also forgive you. But if you do not forgive others their sins, your Father will not forgive your sins. (Matthew 6:14–15)

But we have this treasure in jars of clay to show that that all-surpassing power is from God and not from us. We are hard pressed on every side, but not crushed; perplexed, but not in despair; persecuted, but not abandoned; struck down, but not destroyed. (2 Corinthians 4:7–9)

Each of you should use whatever gift you have received to serve others, as faithful stewards of God's grace in its various forms. (1 Peter 4:10)

About the Author

Molly Beth Photography

S arah Lee is just a simple girl striving to make a positive impact in the kids and other people she encounters. She is a first-grade teacher who enjoys seeing how far a child progresses from the beginning of the year to the end. She has recently opened Woven By Grace, a boutique in Oklahoma. She has become compelled to help others see their worth and learn to love themselves no matter their looks or their past. She can relate to many in the good times but most of all in the seasons of insecurity and doubt. She is a woman who does not live in fear anymore because she knows God is in control.

Sarah lives with her family in Texas and would love to know your story and pray for you. Connect with her on a daily basis, and see pictures of her family and friends.

Facebook: @the.sarah.lee.nwan
Instagram: @the.sarah.lee

CPSIA information can be obtained
at www.ICGtesting.com
Printed in the USA
LVHW112010160420
653663LV00002B/753